International
bill 1 – 1

Improving Teacher Education In the United States

The Report of a Symposium Sponsored Jointly by Phi Delta Kappa International, Stanford University, and the Stanford University Chapter of Phi Delta Kappa

Edited by

STANLEY ELAM

Published by

PHI DELTA KAPPA, *Incorporated*
Eighth Street and Union Avenue
Bloomington, Indiana

Preface

The symposium reported in this volume had its beginnings in an action of the 29th Council of Phi Delta Kappa, held at Lincoln, Nebraska, in December, 1963. Mounting public criticism of teacher education led the council delegates to call for a symposium to examine certain fundamental problems of formal teacher preparation in the United States.

Less than a month later, Horace Aubertine wired me that the Stanford University Chapter of the fraternity, of which he was then president, was interested in holding such a symposium. He submitted a proposal shortly thereafter and the Phi Delta Kappa Board of Directors allocated funds at its February, 1964, meeting to help finance the project.

Planning and preparation took a year and a half, and when the symposium was held, on October 22 and 23, 1965, it proved to be one of the most penetrating and constructive examinations of this vital and much discussed topic that we have witnessed in this decade.

Credit for the success of the symposium must be distributed among many persons, but certain individuals deserve a great deal of it and should be recognized. Mr. Aubertine was succeeded as the Stanford Chapter president by Norman Dodl, who did much of the preliminary work. Jerry Becker followed Mr. Dodl as president in 1965-66 and probably devoted more time and effort to the project than any other person. Without his effective and patient work the symposium would have been much less successful.

The symposium steering committee was composed of Mr. Becker, Robert N. Bush, Nathaniel L. Gage, Richard E. Gross (chapter sponsor), and G. Wesley Sowards. Other individuals who served were Mr. Aubertine, now at Arizona State University; Mr. Dodl, now at the University of Illinois; and Henry Cordes, College of San Mateo.

Phi Delta Kappa officers most closely concerned with the symposium were Edwin A. Swanson, area coordinator who helped with planning; Charles R. Foster, past president who acted for me in the spring of 1964; Arthur E. Arnesen, current president; Homer L. Johnson, president-elect; and J. W. Lee, board members, all of whom attended the symposium. Gordon I. Swanson was president of the fraternity when the project was approved.

Our thanks also go to I. James Quillen, former dean of the Stanford School of Education, for his interest and support.

MAYNARD BEMIS
Executive Secretary
Phi Delta Kappa

October 1, 1966

1966-68 OFFICERS OF PHI DELTA KAPPA

PRINTED IN THE UNITED STATES OF AMERICA

v

SYMPOSIUM PARTICIPANTS

Presenting Major Papers—Harry S. Broudy, Professor of Philosophy of Education, University of Illinois; Robert N. Bush, Professor of Education, Stanford University; Herbert Schueler, Professor of Education and Director of Teacher Education, Hunter College of the City University of New York (now President, Richmond College, City University of New York); Morris L. Cogan, Professor of Education and Chairman, Department of Teacher Education, University of Pittsburgh; Melvin W. Barnes, Superintendent of Public Schools, Portland, Oregon; and James C. Stone, Professor of Education and Director of Teacher Education, University of California, Berkeley.

Session Chairmen—Nathaniel L. Gage, Richard E. Gross, G. Wesley Sowards, Dwight W. Allen, William H. Strand, and Lawrence G. Thomas, all of Stanford University.

Discussion Participants (in addition to persons presenting papers)— Arno A. Bellack, Professor of Education, Teachers College, Columbia University; Norman J. Boyan, Associate Professor of Education, Stanford University; Don Davies, Executive Secretary, National Commission on Teacher Education and Professional Standards, National Education Association; and Gordon M. A. Mork, Professor of Education and Director of Student Teaching, University of Minnesota. (A number of guests and observers also participated in the discussions and are noted by last name where identified by the recorder.)

Table of Contents

Page

Chapter I

The Role of the Foundational Studies In the Preparation of Teachers

By HARRY S. BROUDY
Professor of Philosophy of Education
University of Illinois

I shall begin the discussion of the role of the foundational studies in the preparation of teachers by registering some dissatisfaction with the terms "foundation" and "foundational." The brave band of professors at Columbia Teachers College deserve our gratitude for the idea of foundational studies, but not for the term.

Inevitably the word makes one think of the building trades, or those great philanthropic geese that lay the golden eggs for educational reform, or the art of corsetry. All these connotations have their roots in the notion of a beginning. The foundation of the edifice is the first layer of the building, and when one founds an establishment he institutes or originates it; presumably an establishment is called a foundation when its goal is to assist in the founding of other enterprises. As for the foundation garments worn by ladies, they too are supposed to be the first layer of clothing as well as the means of establishing a basic contour for the figure's subsequent adornment.

Along with the connotation of initiation or beginning goes the idea of importance. What is foundational is supposed to be fundamental, basic, supportive. Without foundations, one is led to believe, there can be no houses, no fashionable figures, no research, no first-class trips on jet airplanes to esoteric conferences, and no innovations in education, especially in teacher education.

1

These images and their penumbral meanings are quite unsatisfactory. To begin with, the foundational studies are rarely first in order of instruction. For the most part, they are reserved for the later phases of teacher preparation. Some schools—as a matter of fact, theory, or convenience—reserve these studies for in-service training or postpone them until after the student has done practice teaching. The delay is urged on the ground that the student will be more mature and consequently more ready for the history, philosophy, and the sociology of education. The psychology of education (or the psychological foundations of education) is an exception, because one expects it to be applied to problems of the classroom, and therefore should precede practice teaching. This is a tribute to the confidence education places in psychology. Whether curriculum makers expect the other foundational studies to help the teacher in the future or merely to appreciate his past training is not always clear. In any event, to call a study "foundational" and to offer it is as the frosting on the cake of the teacher-training program certainly mixes up the metaphors.

In the second place, the metaphor of a foundation as holding something up, as something on which one builds, fails badly when used in connection with educational history and philosophy, and limps even with regard to the psychology and sociology of education. Their placement at various stages of the training indicates that they are not uniformly thought of as prerequisites for later studies that incorporate them as elements. On the contrary, they themselves require (or should require) the study of the parent disciplines of history, psychology, sociology, and philosophy as prerequisites. However, the sciences of education if fully developed might well qualify as prerequisites for large segments of the teacher-preparation curriculum.

THEORY AND PRACTICE

Distracting as foundational imagery may be, it is less damaging than the unrealistic expectations it spawns. Of these hopes two are especially dubious, viz., that courses in the foundations will provide technical solutions to classroom problems, and that

2

they will serve as unambiguous prescriptions of educational policy.

Now it is true that methods of coping with unruly pupils and slow learners are often mentioned in foundational courses. One finds advice from the time of Plato on that harsh corporal punishment is to be avoided, and that its use is a judgment on the teacher rather than the pupil. Quintilian, Comenius, Rousseau, Pestalozzi, and a troop of other pedagogical notables anticipated B.F. Skinner's aversion to learnings motivated by aversion. Nor is the history of education devoid of suggestions as to devices. In the accounts of Alcuin, for example, one finds detailed instructions on the teaching of grammar and an ingenious method for finding the sum of an arithmetical progression.[1]

Nonetheless, one would hardly justify reading Alcuin's educational writings by promising that they will help prospective teachers to teach arithmetic. Nor would one justify the study of the *Principia Mathematica* by Bertrand Russell and Alfred N. Whitehead on these grounds. These studies may have a contribution to make to teacher training, but not as technical handbooks.

As we shall have occasion to observe below, for an inquiry to provide logically justifiable rules of practice it must have

---

[1] A ladder has 100 steps. On the first sits one pigeon, on the second two, on the third three, and so on up to the hundredth. How many pigeons in all?

I once saw Max Wertheimer of Gestalt fame use a variation of this problem to illustrate the tyranny of stereotyped perception and liberation from it by insight. Instead of adding the pigeon (or its number) on the first step to the two on the adjacent step, as virtually everyone does, Wertheimer would suggest that one add 1 to 100, 2 to 99, 3 to 98, etc. At different rates his audience caught on to the solution, viz., that there would be 50 pairs of 101 pigeons.

Alcuin did it a bit differently. He reasoned:

> On step one and step 99 combined sit 100 pigeons, similarly on step two and 98, and so on. Step 50 and 100 have no pairs. So his answer is: 49 times 100 plus 50 plus 100 equals 5050 pigeons." (Eleanor S. Duckett, *Alcuin, Friend of Charlemagne*, New York: Macmillan, 1951, pp. 116-117. Quoted in H. S. Broudy and J. R. Palmer, *Exemplars of Teaching Method*, Chicago: Rand McNally, 1965, p. 51).

Alcuin not only had insight into the use of pairs, but also avoided the need for dealing with the awkward sum of 101 for each pair.

theories from which the phenomena one has to deal with can be deduced. In other words, the inquiry must have the form of an empirical science and a complement of well-established facts, laws, hypotheses, criteria, and modes of investigation. Studies that cannot qualify as empirical sciences should not be expected to yield important rules of practice that will carry scientific warranty. It is important, therefore, to distinguish between those studies in teacher education that are or might become empirical sciences from those that are not and will not be; and it is no less important to distinguish between expecting to use what one learns for application to professional problems from using it for the interpretation of them. I shall argue that there is a place in teacher education for studies that are used primarily for interpretive purposes, and that some of these studies are science-like while others are not.

Let us turn now to the expectation so frequently entertained that the foundational studies will reveal to the prospective teacher clear-cut prescriptions of the good life, the good society, and the good school. A study of democracy, for example, is supposed to enable the student to judge whether a given proposal is or is not democratic. The objections to this kind of claim are generally of two sorts:

1. There are differing philosophies. Either each is consistent with a variety of educational policies or it is not. If they are, there is no point in studying them; if they are not, there is no way to choose among them, for it is argued—wrongly I believe—that they are expressions of attitudes and not empirically verifiable or unverifiable.

2. If one cannot get advice on educational policy from philosophy, one cannot get it from science-like foundational studies either, because science proclaims what *is* the case or what *might be* the case, but not what *ought* to be the case, and that's what educational policy matters are about.

This leaves the hope that the social sciences in time will tell us enough about what *is* the case and what *might be* the case to help us achieve efficiently what we decide *ought* to be the case. This is a legitimate expectation from psychology, sociology, anthropology, and the economics of education, and if for no other reason than this they ought to be studied by pro-

4

spective teachers and indeed by all educational workers regardless of their field of specialization.

Does this mean then that the history and philosophy of education cannot be expected to give guidance in matters of educational valuation? (Objection 1)

On the contrary, precisely because philosophy and so much of history are non-scientific they can and do become sources of value prescription, although rarely in the direct and unambiguous form that some anticipate. These disciplines are nothing if not invitations to belief and commitment. Every philosophical system is an endorsement of a way of life by virtue of its theories about the nature of truth, goodness, and beauty. And no historian is able to avoid by his selection of facts an implicit approval of some events and the deploring of others.

Although neither philosophy nor history can claim to be an empirical science, they do not thereby surrender their claims to cognitive status. The value affirmations within a system of philosophy do make a claim to truth—not empirical but philosophical truth. The evidence for philosophical truth is not an experiment, however well designed, but the fruits of mankind experimenting, reasoning, and arguing about the meaning of what it means to be truly human. The perennial, rational, systematic consideration and reconsideration of what is true, good, and beautiful constitute the cognitive warrant for philosophical discourse. These considerations are to be found in the history of the culture.

That rival theories still exist does not mean that they are the results of caprice, impulse, or superstition; that they are no more than pedantic fairy tales. It means that so far as we as yet know more than one style of life can be judged good; but these no more necessarily negate each other than one fine symphony negates another. Each can be consistent within itself and true to itself logically, morally, and aesthetically. However, rival theories need not be compatible and can negate each other practically as well as contradict each other logically. Strife in the world is a fact; so is strife in theory.

Although the study of the history and the philosophy of education can be a source of beliefs about value and can also provide principles for justifying educational policies, one cannot repeat too often that between general philosophical discussions and proposals for action lie many theoretical and practical booby traps. How to detect these, discuss them, and evade them is itself one of the primary objectives of the philosophy of education.

The expectations of technical skill and policy wisdom from the foundational studies have to be stated with caution—a caution that has not always been prominent in the claims of their advocates. I would want to maintain that the application of theory to practice is not the appropriate justification for the foundational studies, at least not equally so for all of them. Even to verify theory (not to speak of applying it), one needs transformation rules by which the elements in the theory can be turned into experimental variables, e.g., the jumping of electrons from one orbit in an atom into shifts of spectral lines, or the theory of the aether into the Michelson-Morley experiment.[2] But not all verified theories are necessarily applied. Inventiveness that issues in an apparatus and technique is also needed. Model building, one may suppose, not only helps to interpret theory but also furnishes an impetus to imagining applications and inventing technical means of making these applications.

We think with concepts, but we can act only with and on particular existents that are fuzzy with concreteness. As a result, theoretical sophistication may leave the practitioner baffled by the peculiarities of the individual case. However, if individual cases, despite their idiosyncrasies, fall into recognizable classes—and if they are to be at all intelligible they must—rules for dealing with the classes can be formulated and used without explicit invocation of the theory (if any) behind them. Sometimes we achieve good results without anyone knowing the theory that explains them, e.g., the early uses of sulfa drugs.

These facts exert a pressure upon a profession to regress to its craft beginnings from which it cannot and does not wish wholly to escape. Its commerce with particulars distinguishes it from a purely scientific enterprise that thirsts after knowledge only; it is distinguished from a craft by a compulsion to rationalize its procedures by theory. A professional field has to develop

---

[2] Cf. Ernest Nagel, *The Structure of Science*, New York: Harcourt, Brace, and World, 1961, pp. 90 ff.

a technology in order to apply knowledge, but it has also to develop or utilize theory to escape trial-and-error or even trial-and-success empiricism.

STRUCTURE OF A PROFESSIONAL FIELD OF STUDY

The role of the so-called foundational studies in a professional field cannot be truly understood without some theory about the structure of such a field.

First of all, the anchors of a professional field are its problems of practice. These problems not only distinguish it from other professions but also set it off from the intellectual (academic) disciplines that are organized in terms of knowledge about a field of homogeneous objects and principles.

Secondly, because a professional field is designed to cope with problems of practice—problems that arise out of human needs—it tends to draw its knowledge from many disciplines. Some of this knowledge it recruits for the interpretation of its own complex problems, some for inventing a technology of coping with them, and some for crystalizing norms of value that define and justify its activities in the human enterprise. Part of this knowledge the professional is expected to absorb from what is loosely called general education, but much of what is needed does not automatically transfer from general education; as a result, a distinctively professional field of study comes into being.

In time, a professional field is constituted by layers of knowledge, each descending layer coming closer to the particularity of practice. Pharmacology is closer to medical treatment than chemistry; stethoscopy than anatomy. As he goes about helping his flock out of their predicaments, the cleric may find Bible study closer to his tasks than theology; pastoral psychology more immediately relevant than personality theory, and an intimate knowledge of his parishioners (or a knowledge of his parishioners' intimacies) more useful than either.

In some sense all of these layers of knowledge are "applicable" to practice. In view of their being selected precisely for this reason, this is hardly surprising. However, operationally, applicability varies over a wide range—from tricks of the trade to the most abstruse principles of the parent disciplines. Because one

7

can use the tricks and rules, up to a point, without theory, there is perennial war between the student in a professional school and his mentors. The former, eager to practice, would settle for rules and tricks; the latter, representing the field, will permit no such thing, and prescribe substantial doses of theory. The layman watching the behavior of the physician or the teacher quite naturally concludes that with a little apprentice training he could do it himself; that the theoretical requirements are mumbo jumbo devised by the Establishment to keep the membership low and the fees high.

As scientific knowledge develops it becomes increasingly general. To apply it to professional practice requires the straddling of several levels of generality and several areas of knowledge. To apply nuclear physics to cancer therapy calls for men who know a great deal about cancer therapy, not a little about cancer theory, something about the theory and techniques of radiology, and knowledge of the physiological effects of radiation. However, they need not be experts in all of these departments.

For this reason it is misleading to characterize professional knowledge simply as the application of theory. The professional applies theory only in his specialty, but his education cannot be restricted to the theory one thinks he will apply. For we do not know which theories will become relevant to future problems, and furthermore, in order to apply knowledge one must first understand enough about the whole empire of knowledge to make an educated guess as to which region in this vast domain will contain the relevant theory.[3]

If I have belabored this point it is because prospective teachers and some of their professors gauge the value of all profes-

---

[3] The oversimplification of applying theory to practice is abetted by the confusion of logical explanation with application. Logically, a theory T explains phenomenon P, if P is deductible from T, i.e., if P is covered by the generalizations in T, and if certain initial conditions demanded by the theory are satisfied. Thus from the theory of nuclear fission and radioactivity one might predice that certain substances could be made radioactive in nuclear reactors (isotopes). However, the idea of applying this notion to cancer therapy is more likely to occur to a cancer therapist than to a nuclear physicist. Thus although all the potential applications are logically implicit in the theory, in practice the discoveries of applications are not made at the same time nor usually by the same persons.

8

sional studies solely on their power to beat a straight path for them from the general to the particular; from theory to practice; from awkwardness to ease; from uncertainty to confidence. This is a primrose path. The path of virtue is in the opposite direction less alluring, to be sure, but also less likely to bring upon us the recrimination of disillusioned maidens who look vainly in their class notes for help in quelling pupil revolts or dispelling pupil apathy.

THE INTERPRETIVE USE OF KNOWLEDGE

The more modest promise that the philosophy, history, psychology, and the sociology of education can make *at this time* is the interpretive understanding of problems rather than technics for solving them. What is to be meant by interpretation or interpretive understanding?

There is no need to dwell here on the nature and scope of problems properly called educational. Roughly they fall into four areas: 1) formulating and justifying aims and policies, 2) designing and justifying curricula, 3) organizing and rationalizing systems of schooling, and 4) teaching-learning. There is nothing final or sacrosanct about this classification. The important point is that to understand a problem one needs to classify it in some way. The first step in understanding is to locate a problem within some system of meanings. Intellectual disciplines are our most familiar and most useful systems of meaning, but religion, art, and instructional folkways are also important for the interpretation of experience.[4]

A number of familiar metaphors are available to illustrate this categorization. Each intellectual discipline can be regarded as a cognitive map, and to locate a problem on such a map is to interpret it. Or one might think of the various intellectual disciplines as subsystems operating within larger systems yet not wholly integrated with all other subsystems. The pigeonhole metaphor represents a cruder form of categorization. Each domain of meaning can be thought of as a language system for the

---

[4]Cf. Pitirim Sorokin's notion of sociocultural systems as clusters of meaning.

description of a given set of phenomena. For example, economics and sociology can be thought of as languages for describing the phenomena of poverty and cultural deprivation.

The advantage of locating problems within systems of meaning is obvious, for having done so, one can talk and think about the problem with the conceptual resources of the whole system. To understand something is therefore to be able to talk and think about it in terms of a system of concepts related to each other by predetermined routes of thought.

Does it make any difference which language is used in interpretation? The answer to this question is clouded by the different meanings that attach to the word "understanding." The best and clearest test of understanding is application, but if there can be understanding short of application, what does it mean? Some of the criteria are clearly psychological. Feelings of familiarity, as if the person recognized something he already knew, are not uncommon subjective signs of understanding. Often the "aha!" phenomenon so dear to the Gestaltists serves as such a sign. Sometimes understanding is marked by an ability to place oneself in the mind of another by sympathetic imagination.[5] Clarity, illumination, feelings of release are all cited as indications that something has been understood.

Some of the criteria for interpretive understanding are logical. We can say that X is understood when one discerns the scheme of relations of which X is a part or in which it is embedded. Thus we understand a mathematical X when we discern the system of deductive relations that enables us to infer conclusions from axioms, postulates, previously proved theorems, etc. A system of causes and effects is another logical pattern, evolution is another, and so is any steady sequence. A very important structure is that of means-ends. In short, we understand X interpretively when we can describe 1) the system of meanings

[5]Cf. The notion of *Verstehende Soziologie* advocated by Ludwig von Mises in *Theory and History* (New Haven: Yale University Press, 1957) and the "methodological individualism" of F. A. Hayek in *The Counter Revolution in Science* (Glencoe, Ill.: The Free Press, 1955).

in which it is embedded and 2) when we discern the position of X in this system, i.e., relate it to other elements of the system.

Hence the current emphasis in education on the logical structure of subject matter is sound, especially if understanding is the goal of instruction. It lies at the root of whatever transfer we hope to claim for a study. However, because the state of the learner's knowledge is peculiar to himself, pedagogically the understanding of X may require more than a decision to make him aware of the logical properties of a system of meanings. For example, the level of abstraction within such a system may be too high for the learner, and the work of Piaget would seem to point to this possibility. To interpret X might therefore mean translating it into a more concrete language, i.e., language which is more descriptive of the gross characteristics of phenomena: of rows of pebbles rather than the numbers that are used to describe their order. Sometimes a metaphor, an example, an embedding of the X into the experience sequences of the learner will be the most effective interpretants. That a logical system of meanings is the most effective matrix of interpretation is undeniable. An interpretation that incorporates X into a system with a greater potential for generality than the one in which it subsists in the mind of the learner is cognitively better than one that does not; the wider the context the greater the cognitive flexibility and freedom of the knower, because the routes of continuity are thereby multiplied and their direction clarified.

Getting the pupil ready to interpret in the languages of the diverse disciplines is no less important than having him do so, and that is why studies that teachers need for interpretation of their pedagogical problems are not simply the academic disciplines themselves. And for the same reason, simple updating of the classroom teacher in the standard disciplines will not automatically enable him to produce growth of understanding in the pupil. To accomplish the pedagogical task the teacher will need to interpret it and execute it. The foundational studies will be required for interpretation of the task, but may not be sufficient for its execution. This difference in uses of knowledge is not confined to teaching. For example, many of us can understand the workings of the internal combustion engine without being

11

able to fix the one in our automobile. Our interpretive ability in matters of health and disease does not appreciably lower our doctor bills.[6]

Humanistic and Scientific "Foundations"

The systems of meaning and language in which educational problems can be understood are as numerous as the fields of human knowledge itself, for nothing human is alien to education. Nevertheless, some languages are more immediately relevant than others. The languages of the disciplines dealing with human behavior are more directly relevant to education than those dealing with the behavior of gases.

We could, one might suppose, arrange all knowledge on a continuum of relevance-immediacy to problems of education. At one end of such a continuum would be the most general fields of philosophy, and at the other might be the procedural rules for specific problems. Roughly this continuum could be divided into three segments: 1) interpretive studies, 2) interpretive-applicational studies, and 3) technological studies and technical exercises.

The middle group is pivotal to the other two. It is in this layer that one hopes to develop the interdisciplinary bodies of professional theory by which one can explain the phenomena one is dealing with; and on the basis of which one can invent the appropriate technology for applying the theory to practice. Educational measurement is an example of such an interdisciplinary field.

Hence, as the middle section develops, there is a tendency for the interpretive studies to separate into those that are scientific (psychology, sociology, anthropology, and economics), on the one hand, and those that are humanistic, (history, philosophy, art) on the other. Both can be used for interpretation by all workers in the field, and as so used they constitute the general study of education. However, insofar as the middle

---

[6]For a more detailed discussion of the uses of knowledge, cf. H. S. Broudy, B. Othanel Smith, and Joe R. Burnett, *Democracy and Excellence in American Secondary Education*, Chicago: Rand McNally, 1964, Chapters 3 and 4.

group of scientific studies are used as a source and justification of technology, they tend to attach themselves to technological studies and become part of the field of specialization.[7] Thus, test construction for a junior high school algebra course is part of one's field of specialization.

This is not the place to discuss in detail the theoretical obstacles that bar the way of the social "sciences" into the empyrean realms of physics and chemistry.[8] The obstacles are real, and it ill behooves us to behave as if they were already surmounted. The fact of the matter is that in the social sciences many of the findings are no more than formalized statements of common sense, although some are so complex that they conceal whatever is common or sensible in them. Nevertheless, we should not underestimate the power of the computer to deal with complexity.[9]

More significant is the lack of a solid core of "fact" and well-established theory to serve as nuclei and criteria for research. As a result much research is accumulating about all sorts of educational problems, but the results are strangely noncumulative.

HUMANISTIC FOUNDATIONS

At this point one is faced with the temptation of doing away with all non-empirical "general" studies. This eventuality has been devoutly desired by those who regard the humanities as a poor substitute for the social sciences in human engineering.

However, we may recall what was said earlier about the role of history and philosophy as sources of value prescription.

---

[7] Courses of this kind make possible "laboratory" experience in the professional curriculum.

[8] Nagel, op. cit., Chapters 13 and 14.

[9] It is instructive to go through Human Behavior, by Bernard Berelson and Gary A. Steiner, (New York: Harcourt, Brace and World, 1964), which undertakes to inventory the "findings" of the social sciences. As examples of formalized common sense consider the following: "When a person is frustrated the barrier may be attacked physically or symbolically . . . if actual attack is impossible aggression may be displaced to an innocent but more vulnerable bystander." (p. 267) "Strong informal groups within an organization, when hostile to its goals and methods, can effectively oppose the organization." (p 372)

13

Those for whom the term "knowledge" is restricted to the generalizations of the empirical sciences are naturally doubtful about the values of the humanities. For if they reflect cultural prejudices that cannot be justified rationally, they are socially incompatible with a free society and cognitively they are frauds: myths parading as truths.

On this view, to be human is to be nonrational, albeit sensible, about values, and the role of the humanities as value arbiters would be taken by the social sciences; these disciplines at least describe accurately the ultimate values a population holds without making any pretense to answering the question: Are these values worthy of being held? The humanities, however, depend on the belief that philosophical answers to this question are in some sense knowledge, and that art in some sense exhibits value examplars in a significant way.[10] The humanistic studies for interpretive understanding of educational problems cannot be replaced by scientific studies, for their own results need interpretation.

It should be clear from the history of thought that the empirical sciences differ from the humanities in their modes of inquiry, types of concern, and canons of adequacy. Even when philosophy restricts itself with pious austerity to the canons of logic and talks only about empirical science, it is not itself an empirical science. Academic degrees in philosophy of science and in any one of the sciences are not identical, however little or much the requirements for them may overlap. Doing science and talk about the doing of science are not quite the same thing. So the prospect of doing away with philosophy altogether by converting it into a science is still not good.

As for history, its scientific aspirations are notoriously vain, albeit not wholly in vain. If it cannot give explanations of the type admired in physics and chemistry, it can give genetic explanations, and it can be admirably severe with its own methods and criteria. If it cannot be used for direct application to life or education, it is impossible to interpret either significantly

---

[10]Cf. H. S. Broudy, "The Structure of Knowledge in the Arts," in *Education and the Structure of Knowledge*, Stanley Elam, ed., Fifth Annual Phi Delta Kappa Symposium on Educational Research. Chicago: Rand McNally, 1964, Chapter 3.

without it. Hence the prospect of history becoming absorbed wholly into the empirical sciences is not much brighter than that of the abolition of philosophy.

Thus we can anticipate that philosophy of education will retain what is now known as the philosophy of man or philosophical anthropology, some philosophical psychology and social and political philosophy, leaving to the sciences of education the more clearly empirical inquiries into the sociology, economics, anthropology, and politics of education, but not abdicating from its role as the interpreter of their methods and results. This may do away with Social Foundations of Education courses which try to combine the philosophical and the empirical disciplines, but their humanistic content will be taken over by courses in the history and philosophy of education. In the same way, the psychological foundations of education may split into psychology as educational science on the one hand and educational philosophy on the other (philosophical psychology).

The problem of deciding who shall do what in these areas is a more difficult issue. It is argued in some prestigious quarters that if there are to be either humanities of education or sciences of education, the academic scholars in the respective parent disciplines should write the books and give the courses. We are seeing an increasing effort to persuade economists, sociologists, philosophers, and historians to turn their professional competence to the field of education.[11] The argument seems to run something like this: The very best thing that could happen would be to have the teacher-training curriculum which has been developed by professors of education in schools of edu-

---

[11] Publishers, some of the philanthropic foundations, and college of education administrators seeking academic respectability for their threatened institutions are often zealous participants in this effort. Part of the campaign involves offering joint appointments to such scholars as can be lured away from their academic specialities. This maneuver helps to show the world that the college of education is being run with the help of respectable academicians and not by the educationists. An even better ploy is to ask the department of history or philosophy or psychology to give a joint appointment to staff members of the college of education. This is a very satisfying form of certification both to the staff member and the college of education, and that it does so furnishes all the comment that is necessary on the professional status of these institutions.

15

cation sunk far out at sea. One could then train liberal arts graduates for teaching by means of a brief but intensive internship with master teachers or clinical professors. Master teachers presumably are thrown up every so often as sports in the evolutionary process, and one can spot them although one can't really train them. If the very best thing cannot be brought off (due to the strength of the educationist establishment), and if there must be courses labeled "education," then we should exile the professors of education and call in the academic specialists to do what needs to be done. Economists doing the economics of education and philosophers doing philosophy of education would make the so-called foundational courses tolerable although not necessary.

Unfortunately, just as not all professors of physics are interested or competent in engineering, and just as not all biologists are interested in or competent to teach anatomy or pathology, just as not all historians are historians of law or medicine, so not all academic specialists are ready or willing to exercise their special expertise on problems of education.

For it is the nature of a professional field of study to be oriented toward and organized by its problems of practice, and not by the parent disciplines from which it draws some of its theoretical sustenance. These problems are familiar and intelligible only to those who have invested time, study, and concern in them. Any given professor of economics may have made this investment, but in this age of specialization the odds are pretty much against it. Hence, even when persuaded to play the role of savior of education his contributions tend to be expressed in language that the educational practitioner cannot understand or couched in principles so general and abstract that it takes an educationist to interpret their import for educational theory and practice.

The more realistic solution is, of course, the harder one. It is to recognize that good professors of the science or the humanities of education are rarer than either the academic subject matter specialist or the classroom practitioner. Their models are to be sought in the schools of engineering, medicine, and law where similar hard-to-come-by combinations of practice and theory are also needed and command high salaries.

16

One may righteously share the indignation of the volunteer saviors of education with philosophers of education who are inept in philosophy and historians of education who are not well prepared in history. But academicians whose knowledge of education is limited by their own schooling or by that which they are providing for their own students or by their membership in the PTA are not the answer either.

A Design for Professional Curriculum

If my analysis of the situation is at all plausible, then the curriculum for teacher preparation could look something like this:

GENERAL PROFESSIONAL STUDIES FOR INTERPRETIVE USE

Humanistic studies of education in general
    History of education (including cultural history of education)
    Philosophy of education
    Aesthetic education
Scientific studies of (or sciences) of education
    Psychology of education
    Sociology of education
    Economics of education
    Anthropology of education

PROFESSIONAL STUDIES IN THE FIELD OF SPECIALIZATION FOR APPLICATION

Humanistic backgrounds of one's specialty
Technology of one's specialty
    Theoretical studies (contributions of sciences to practice)
    Technical rules of procedure
    Clinical work and internship
    Methods for production and consumption of research

17

Schematized in this way, the word "foundation" drops out, to be replaced by "general" or "interpretive," and this difference, I believe, is more than semantic. For one thing, it avoids the connotational difficulties of the foundational metaphors. "General" and "interpretive" do not conjure up visions of the building trades and corsetry. More important, they do not carry the connotation of being prerequisites for everything else in the curriculum, although one might wish to give them this priority. Above all, the terms "general" and "interpretive" do not set up unwarranted expectations of applicability.

The words "general" and "interpretive" go together in that one can recommend interpretive studies for all teachers and educational professionals. The reason for this is that a professional applies knowledge directly only in his specialty, yet as a professional he needs to understand the educational enterprise as a whole. He needs this not only for general sophistication, but to understand his own specialty's role in that enterprise. The science of education as bearing on his own specialty is embodied in the technology of his specialty.

The Role of the General or Interpretive Studies

The theme of this essay can now be restated as follows: What can we expect from nonspecialized work in the preparation of teachers? If teacher preparation goes beyond apprenticeship, special methods, and techniques, in what shall it consist, and how does one justify what is to be included?

In the light of the discussion on the applicative and interpretive uses of knowledge, it seems clear that interpretation rather than application is the primary justification for general studies. These are a necessary but not a sufficient condition for application. To be sufficient they would have to be supported by and translated into technology.

I have tried to show that empirical sciences of education have the greatest potential for this. Even when not translated into a technology, these "sciences of education" provide all educational workers with the cognitive categories, maps, and languages by which to systematize their thinking and talking about the problems that are common to the field as a whole and to their own specialty.[12] They need these studies as members of the profession, not as persons or educational specialists.

Although history does not furnish exact replications of instances, so that scientific generalizations in the ordinary sense of that term cannot be expected from it, yet the instances are not so unique as to be incomparable. Previous attempts, for example, to use formal schooling to redeem underprivileged children are not identical, to be sure, but that they are completely unrelated only the most austere and obstinate skeptics would assert. Not only does the ignorance of history condemn us to repeating it; it also generates unseemly claims to originality on the part of educational reformers.

Philosophy of education furnishes cognitive maps that differ from those afforded by the empirical sciences. The languages of epistemology, metaphysics, aesthetics, and logic are distinctive languages. They are very general, but they do clarify the meanings of and relationships among concepts; so in the end nothing really escapes their net. Especially important is that aspect of philosophy which deals with the criteria of knowledge itself, for here are the tools for a most important type of interpretation.

---

[12]Although this is not the place to develop the point, something should be said about what in the schema is called the humanistic backgrounds of one's specialty. Having studied the history and philosophy of general educational problems, why, it may be asked, should a potential school administrator study the history and philosophy of school administration? Or why should a prospective mathematics teacher study the history and philosophy of mathematics teaching?

The simple answer is that the general courses cannot give detailed attention to the specialties. The more signficant answer, I believe, takes a somewhat different tack. I am thinking of the wide variety of courses that are used to introduce the teacher to the field of specialization. They include everything from orientation lectures to the methods of teaching. Much of the bitterness about the repetitiveness of education courses issues from this introductory course, parts of which are likely to find their way into every course and textbook in education.

Yet what better introduction to a specialty can there be than its history and the principles by which its theories and values are given their rationale? But it has to be more than a perfunctory statement on the importance of education in general and of the specialty in particular. Whereas the general history and philosophy of education work has to be given by philosophers and historians of education, the humanistic aspects of specialty should be given by the specialist who teaches the specialty and is part of the student's specialized study.

19

Reference has already been made to the long controversy as to whether or not facts can yield value judgments; whether or not from what *is* we can deduce what ought to be; whether from reliable information about causes of belief and action we can derive educational policy. This controversy is closely related to the one about the possibility of values being objective. Both controversies are of prime importance to education, because education is about what some one thinks *ought* to be the good life and the kind of learning that will produce it. It cannot escape the value judgment by retreating into fact, especially if the controversy persists despite agreement on fact.

The usefulness of the philosophy of education lies not in its possessing a private certitude about what ought to be the good life but in explicating the categories, the concepts, the language in which to talk about these problems critically, synoptically, and systematically. The history of philosophy displays the great exemplars of systems of ideas about truth, goodness, and beauty in terms of which our civilization has made and justified its value commitments.

In this sense, styles in philosophizing stress different aspects of the field. Linguistic analysis concentrates on the clarification of the meanings of terms used in philosophizing about education.[13] Philosophers of science concentrate on the formal characteristics of scientific thought. The more traditionally styled philosophies explicate various systematic positions with respect to theories of truth and value.

Yet none of these eludes a commitment as to what is good, what is truly true, and what is really important. The scientist can with some plausibility *qua* scientist evade the question: Is this goal worthy of being pursued? He can elude it by pleading that his discipline is not competent to deal with it. The philosopher cannot escape it so easily. His discipline must at the very least clarify the question itself. But what does it mean to clarify the question? It means, among other things, that one must decide whether or not it is a sensible question, and this is a way of saying that question ought or ought not to be raised.

---

[13]H. S. Broudy, "The Role of Analysis in Educational Philosophy," *Educational Theory*, October, 1964, pp. 261-69, 285.

Philosophy, philosophy of education, and the history of both philosophy and of education yield cognitive and evaluational maps. They provide or claim to provide intellectual means of dealing with values: the intellectual means of talking and thinking about the ultimate questions of truth, goodness, and beauty. The value component of human life, however, is more than talk about it; it is the having and cherishing experience in a special way. These modes of having and cherishing are sometimes exhibited in the personalities of great men; some are exhibited in works of literature and the other fine arts. That is why both in general education and in the general studies of education there must be a place for not only history, philosophy, and science, but also the fine arts in their relation to life and to the educational enterprise.

The late Harold Rugg tried to establish the aesthetic foundations of education, but only now are the prospects fairly bright for doing so. These studies combine formal aesthetics with problems of education in the arts and of the role of art in education. They deal with works of art as well as theories of art, and insofar as research in the teaching of the arts comes to anything, they will have to deal with it also. Hence it is better to regard aesthetic education as a separate humanistic general study of education rather than a subdivision of the philosophy of education.

In conclusion, I would like to stress that the general interpretive studies which one might reasonably require of all teachers are fashioned with the help of the intellectual disciplines that ought to be part of every human being's general education, but are not identical with them. Part of the complaints about the "foundational" courses is due to the fact that students have not had or do not recall the understandings in history, economics, anthropology, philosophy, sociology, and psychology, not to speak of the fine arts, that their stay at the liberal arts college is supposed to have provided. When the student is not ready—and until colleges of education are truly autonomous professional schools they cannot demand this readiness—there is a temptation to turn the foundation course into a watered-down version of the parent discipline, or into windy class discussions of life in general, education in general, and society in general, in short, into a bull session given for credit. The more fully developed a pro-

21

fessional curriculum becomes, the less can it be substituted for general education and vice versa.

Nor would I make a claim for the general interpretive studies on the ground that they will make the teacher a better person. The teacher should be a good person because he is a human being, and not because he is a teacher. Charm is a lovable asset in any person, but when it becomes a vocational requirement—as in being an airline stewardess—it has lost its amateur status, so to speak, and belongs to the professional curriculum. But education for personal development is a duty of general education and not of professional training. That history, philosophy, and aesthetics of education might be useful as part of anyone's general education is worth considering, but this is not the place to do so.

If there is any justification for the general professional studies, it is a professional justification, viz., that they are essential to being a first-rate professional, not to a scholar as scholar nor to a craftsman. They are essential for the understanding and interpretation of the educational enterprise as a whole as well as of one's specialty. Although they are not used applicatively, they are not on that account useless.

Discussion of the Broudy Paper

DAVIES: Arno Bellack will open the discussion by responding to Mr. Broudy's paper.

BELLACK: First of all, it seems to me significant that Mr. Broudy took the approach that he did, setting the problems in the context of a professional appeal, in contrast to a position that is currently fashionable in some quarters; namely, to look toward the development of a discipline of education. Mr. Broudy focused on the professional problem and looked for analogies in medicine and engineering rather than in the academic disciplines such as sociology and psychology. I think this is a very important distinction to make, because the work that is going on in some quarters would lead one in quite different directions. The result of focusing on the profession of education leads one to examine the problems of practice that are distinctive to our field as a profession. In dealing with these problems of practice, we may draw on knowledge from a variety of fields, including the sciences and the humanities, as Mr. Broudy indicated.

An important point stressed by Mr. Broudy is that knowledge can be arranged on a continuum of relevance to the problems of education: first of all, the interpretive studies; secondly, the interpretive-applicational studies, that is, studies leading to application; and then, third, the technological studies and technical exercises. Now, as he suggested, the middle group—that is, the applicational-interpretive studies—is pivotal to the other two. And it seems to me that here one would hope to develop these professional interdisciplinary bodies of theory that would help us explain the phenomena with which we are concerned and help solve problems of practice.

23

I'm going to talk principally about that middle area; but first I would also like to say something very briefly about the interpretive studies that Mr. Broudy talked about.

One of the things we might bear in mind here is that it is not merely a matter of applying the foundational studies to the problems of teaching and learning. Rather, one might desirably look toward the development of reciprocity between these fields. That is, the basic fields themselves can profit from contact with the problems of education. I am reminded, for example, of what R. S. Peters said with reference to those psychologists who are interested in learning theory. It was his contention that at the present time learning theorists have very little to say to educators, but that learning theorists themselves could very well profit by more careful examination of the situations and conditions under which learning and teaching actually go forward in the institutional context of the school.

I would like to focus attention primarily on the second phase, which seems to me to be pivotal, as Mr. Broudy indicated, because here we look toward development of the theoretical notions that will help guide practice. Traditionally, in programs of teacher education we focus on the high-level abstractions or, on the other hand, on the purely empirical tricks of the trade. What has been lacking has been this intermediate phase that is really crucial and central to the problem of developing a professional outlook.

This new range of concerns requires the attention of those of us who work in the sciences of education and the humanities of education. I think we know in general what is required here, but the specific requirements are not very clear. In essence, what we are trying to develop is a new breed of educators, a group concerned with the development of theories related directly to the specialized tasks of the teacher. Obviously, the specialization of the teacher is to teach, and this calls for the development of theories of teaching along the lines already suggested by a few individuals.

Let me give you an example or two to indicate what I have in mind. Nate Gage writes about the importance of developing not *a* theory of teaching but *theories* of teaching dealing with teaching of various bodies of subject matter. Similarly, Jerome Bruner urges that we begin thinking about a theory of instruction that would include among its components notions of structure, sequence, predispositions to learning, patterns of reward and punishment, and the like.

What I am suggesting here is that with respect to the preparation of teachers the interpretive-applicational studies are central and that these studies involve the development of theories dealing with the problems of teaching. Some of the work that is currently under way in research on teaching suggests directions in which we might well move, and in the development of such research those who call themselves scientists of education have a crucial role to play. It would be well if at least some of these individuals would concern themselves not only with the interpretive sphere but also with this second phase, that is, the interpretive-applicational studies.

BARNES: It is sometimes useful, I think, to distinguish between teaching as a professional pursuit, on one hand, and the field of education as a realm of study which might be called a discipline.

BOYAN: I would like to ask whether the full range of studies which Mr. Broudy talked about is really necessary and relevant for all who pursue a program in teacher preparation. I suggest that it is wasteful and unnecessary to expose all people who go into teaching to the full range of preparation, because so many of them stay in teaching for such a short time. Perhaps we should make a much more serious effort than we do to distinguish between the minimum amount of preparation, both education and training, necessary for the transient teacher and the optimum amount necessary for the career teacher. Many of the things which most of us hope for as optimum elements in teacher preparation should really be reserved for the careerist after he has made and demonstrated his commitment to pursue teaching as a career.

I would have very little argument with the particular organization of the general interpretive studies that Mr. Broudy has paraded for us. I think he has done a most admirable job in helping us to distinguish between the interpretive and scientific foundations, although he does not want to use the term, "foundations." Again, I would like to focus some of our attention on the distinction between the preparation of the beginner and the short-term teacher and the preparation for the careerist afer he has made—and it is clear that he has made—a commitment to continue to practice in the field.

STONE: Traditionally, we've thought about the professional preparation of a teacher as involving the foundations of education, curriculum and instruction, plus the opportunity for the person to go out and see a student once in awhile or a lesson demonstrated to a group of students. And then we've culminated this professional preparation with student teaching. The presentation this morning gives us a chance to substitute some new names for these various pieces in the traditional curriculum. In place of foundations we now have "interpretive studies." In place of C and I, with some observation and participation, we have "interpretive application." And in place of student teaching experience, we have "application."

Related to Mr. Boyan's point, it seems to me that I worry about the same sort of problem that he does in looking at these pieces. As some of you will probably see if you stick around tomorrow morning, I would turn Mr. Broudy's components around in the professional preparation of a teacher. I'd start out with "application-interpretation," reversing his theory-application idea. I would have "application" follow. (This is where I would recommend something like an internship or similar intensive experience for all teachers.) After this initial, realistic teaching exposure, I would end with "the interpretive studies" as a capstone to give significance and meaning to the whole experience.

BUSH: I would like to comment on the problem of applicability. Assume that my question is in the context of 10 minutes of eulogy in appreciation for your presentation, Mr. Broudy, as I thought it was excellent. Your suggestion that we eliminate the word "foundation" and substitute "general" is a helpful one, I think, provided it is *not* used to let you off the spot with regard to the question that we're always asking about, namely, applicability. You gave us a neat three-stage classification of

26

humanistic studies and the behavioral sciences, but you did not, I thought, come fully to grips with the problem of applicability. I felt that you wanted in the foundations to be interpretive and speculative and leave to someone else the more difficult task of translating this into professional behavior. This is really the crucial question. We argue about it here at Stanford. Some say that they want their material to be applicable and try so to translate it. Others say, "That's not my business. I'm to be thoughtful and interpretive and it's up to the trainee to make that transfer in some way between what you learn from me and how you subsequently teach."

BROUDY: As regards Mr. Bellack's remarks on the professional approach versus the discipline approach, whether you call it a discipline is partly a problem of semantics. The substantive question is operational, and here again I think one can only look at a profession and ask whether or not the way it uses knowledge is the way in which knowledge is used in a subject such as chemistry or physics or history. I think there's a general agreement that the materials are not organized in the same way. Since all professional problems are molar problems—that is, they involve concrete problems—a great many disciplines are relevant to them. Today one of the major questions is "How does one carry on interdisciplinary thinking about molar problems?" Usually, we get five specialists and put them in a room together. They give five papers, remark, "Well that was a stimulating discussion," and go home.

The point is that a real specialist talks in a special language. To understand two specialist one needs to speak two languages. Interdisciplinary thinking creates a third language in which to express the first two. It is not to be taken for granted that merely putting specialists in the same room will create the metalanguage.

I agree with Mr. Bellack that education, like medicine, engineering, etc., is a cornucopia which draws on a variety of disciplines which are organized for scholarship and for further research; with their own principles of investigation, their own data, their own entities, their own relations. That is how we can tell one discipline from another. I doubt that the study of education has anything unique save its problems.

27

Those who are thinking of education as a discipline, viz., that the study of education can become another discipline, are not wholly in the wrong, because one can stand off and say, "Here are some people who are engaged in education. Let's study what they do." In time one might develop a discipline that organizes knowledge about one domain of problems. One might therefrom get scientific generalizations, for example, about the good teacher, from scholars who are scientists in education, who study systematically what people in education do and say. What they discover can become part of the training of the professional educator, which is far broader than the science of education.

I don't know how a person who is trained in the humanistic foundations of education can do very much to help scholars who would be developing the middle section, the applicational field. Philosophers of education cannot say, "Here are the ends, you go find the means." On the other hand, when the people in the middle area do propose solutions, or do propose theories from which solutions could be derived, then it would be the business of the philosopher of education to appraise those in the light of criteria that are philosophical. This, it seems to me, is what philosophers have always done. They even might, on occasion, come up with a suggestion that would, in turn, serve as a hypothesis, which in turn might serve as a guide to people to go *do* something. For example, although the differences we have noted between interpretive and applicative uses of knowledge are not very original or profound, nevertheless if psychologists would tell us more about what goes on when people apply knowledge and when they interpret, this would help to clarify many problems in curriculum theory. Or the philosopher might point to the need for certain kinds of research. For example, how does a person come to have an authentic judgment in the field of aesthetics? We know almost everything about this problem except the facts. So I am not sure that the nonempirical inquiries are going to have too much directly to say to the researcher except in general criticism, occasional suggestions, and an indication of shortages, lacks, imbalances—that sort of thing.

28

DAVIES: Which would be something.

BROUDY: Yes, it would be if anyone would listen to them, and maybe we would listen to them, if they'd stop making believe they're scientists and technologists.

Now I turn to Mr. Boyan's question and also the one by Mr. Stone: Is the full range of studies necessary for transients? The answer is obviously no. But this is where the battle starts. This is where the chips are down. This is where, to use another cliché, we either fish or cut bait. Let me give you an example that all of you, I think, are familiar with, because I think most of you read *Time Magazine*. And I take it you read it to find out what is the newest thing in education. A few months ago in Detroit a young rascal was arrested for practicing medicine without having a degree, without having passed the medical board examinations; he had taken only sporadic work in graduate school and did even that informally. However, his patients testified that he was one of the best doctors they knew. He was earning over $30,000 or $40,000 a year. I waited with bated breath to hear certain personages in our field come out with a blast against a wasteful medical course which takes up six or seven years when here's a chap who did it all quite informally. I have asked physicians: "How many of your patients would get well if you did nothing, if they could manage to stagger into your office?" The percentage runs between 55 to 75 per cent. And if you ask, "How many could imitate what a physician does by giving placebos or kindly advice or telling patients to sleep better, to come to terms with their wives, eat sensibly, and take exercise?" they admit that a great many people could carry on the practice of medicine successfully by sheer imitation. Why didn't the American Medical Association say, "Here is a new development. We need more doctors. Get rid of all this theory. An A.B. degree and a little internship are enough." The answer is obvious and my answer is equally so. We could, however, choose to train teachers by apprenticeship; indeed, we have done so.

The cost, however, is not within our choice. If you believe seriously that in the next 25 years education is going to be *the* big business, *the* growth industry of our time, then you will hesitate to let teaching become a part-time, transitory occupation without definitely and clearly marking these transients as apprentices or technicians or aides or something of that kind. If one of these apprentices comes out of a "good" school, out of a "good" liberal arts college, that does not change his apprentice status. If there is no structure to the field of education, if we cannot develop a body of theory from which our technology (and I'm going to speak of that in a moment) can be derived, then let's stop playing games and admit teaching is an apprentice field. But if we do this, let's stop making noises about professional training.

I want to comment on a slightly different point that Mr. Stone made. It's not a point to which I really addressed myself, namely, the sequence of the interpretative and the applicative studies. Part of the connotation of "foundation" is that it comes first. There *seems* to be no way of building the house first and the foundation last, but there really is a way. You might assemble your house up in the air from a helicopter and later build the foundation. I don't know what the exact sequence should be because part of the interpretive scheme presumably has already been built into prospective teachers by general education. If they have studied economics, they already have interpretive categories in which to interpret their problems in a certain way, e.g., the problem of the culturally disadvantaged.

As to the specific kinds of interpretive thinking that we use in professional study of problems of education, namely, problems of curriculum, problems of aims and policies, administration, teaching-learning, the sequence depends on when you want students to be able to structure these problems with some precision and rigor. Should interpretive studies come before or after practice teaching? There's such a mess, as far as the entry point into teaching is concerned, that it is hard to prescribe a sequence. But suppose one could imagine the entry point standardized. Then it certainly would seem to make sense to me that the processes of identifying the existential problems and interpreting them would precede practicing their solution. I tend to believe one can't practice fruitfully without interpreting the task intelligently.

30

Now on the last topic, applicability. I can weasel out of this one because I don't think the educational psychologists have yet told us what applicability entails. The only way I can get at this is to ask myself, "What do other people do when they apply knowledge?" Now, I don't propose to bring coals to Newcastle or teach grandmothers to suck eggs, but let me suggest that one can apply a rule of procedure (a) by knowing what the rule is and (b) simply identifying a situation as an instance of the rule. How does one identify an instance of the rule? How does one identify, for example, the knocking in the motor as an instance of a bad sparkplug or a broken piston? One way of doing it is to listen for certain perceptible signs. Then one could say, "If it sounds like this, perform this test with an instrument. Here's the instrument. If the gauge says 70 or more, tell the man he needs a new car. If it's less than 70, tell him something else." Notice that the kind of knowledge needed for this type of application is important, but that it is not at a very high intellectual level. You have to know what a gauge is; you have to know how to use it; you have to be able to infer from perceptible signs that certain conditions obtain.

What happens when someone comes in with a car that sounds like this, but doesn't act on the gauges the way it should? What rules do you apply now? The rule is, "Call the foreman." He may have run across one of these anomalies, and can solve the problem by applying a rule derived from a wider context of experience. Suppose we have a case that baffles the foreman. Do you go out front and ask the sales manager? No. You call in an automotive engineer. What does the automotive engineer have that the others have not? Wider experience? Very doubtful. But he has a theory. He understands, we say, how the thing is put together, and he has hypotheses concerning the causes of anomalous behavior in motor cars. Where does he get the theory? He gets it from a higher level of theory, does he not? What does he *apply* that the mechanic doesn't *apply*? His application is not the testing of a rule, it's the testing of a hypothesis with all that goes with it, especially a device for translating concepts into operations.

There is, it seems to me, more than a difference in degree between application when one does not possess a theory and has

31

only rules, and when one *does* possess a theory. However, common to all cases of application is a technology which translates the theory into ways of manipulating something for producing observable results. Taken etymologically, technology is the *logos* of techné, namely, the rationalization of practice, and is largely the result of inventiveness. One needs an intimate acquaintance with the phenomena if a theory is to be applied. The development of a technology doesn't happen just because one has a theory. One needs a deep familiarity with the problems of practice before the possibility of applying the theory can occur.

BUSH: Your analogy is most interesting. I see a new and, perhaps, more productive use of the foundational people to teach those people who are the most difficult learning problems in schools. You could take all of the learning problems that are the most difficult. As the analogy of the difficult car problem suggests, take the problem cases off the hands of the regular teachers, let the greatest theoreticians teach then. Would this be an accurate interpretation of your analogy?

BROUDY: No, because foundations people don't have the technology to apply theory to special problems.

BUSH: What we want to advance, I presume, is the state of our practice.

BOYAN: We do this to a certain extent when we refer a person to the clinical psychologist or to the psychiatrist or eventually to another institution. I suspect we used to distinguish between and among behavior problems. Are we talking about learning in the sense of learning mathematics or science or biology, or learning in the sense of personal and social behavior?

BROUDY: I don't quite get the point of your question. Would you mind repeating it?

BUSH: I think what we are probing for is this: Does the way in which the foundational material is presented to the prospective practitioner make a difference in how well he is able to make the important link between what he learns in preparation and his eventual practice?

BROUDY: I tried to argue that this is exactly what you cannot expect the humanistic foundations to do. If this is to be done, it will be done by the embryonic behavioral sciences which will generate the kind of empirical theory from which technologies can be developed by suggestion and invention.

BELLACK: Now, where does one put the classroom teacher? That is, where is the classroom teacher, one who knows only the rules, in contrast to someone such as the supervisor or principal, who is concerned with theory?

BROUDY: I think it almost follows, doesn't it, Mr. Bellack, that the teacher as a specialist, whatever the specialty of the teacher is, should be able to apply theory? But in all areas outside of his specialty he should be able to use knowledge interpretatively.

BELLACK: So it's not just the rules.

BROUDY: No. Unless you want to settle for a technician.

ADJOURNMENT

Chapter II

The Science and Art of Educating Teachers

By Robert N. Bush
Professor of Education
School of Education
Stanford University

Introduction

In the upward struggle of teachers to become professional, the emphasis has been more upon the *art* than upon the *science* of teaching. This imbalance is in process of redress. As attention to the scientific realm increases, new dangers and opportunities arise. Much of what follows draws upon efforts at Stanford to improve the technical side of teacher training. While we need to continue, even to accelerate this endeavor, a new and equally vigorous thrust should be mounted along artistic and humanistic lines.

Evidence accumulates that professional training does make a difference in preparing teachers. Specific training on particular aspects of teaching can be accomplished, both for beginning and experienced teachers, without destroying the artistry, individuality, and creativity of teachers; it can even enhance these attributes. I am inclined to doubt that genuine artistry in teaching can develop without a thorough underpinning of scholarly, scientific study and training in many of the specific aspects of teaching. An analogy from the field of modern painting comes to mind. Many of the late nineteenth and twentieth century painters with established worldwide reputations in impressionist and abstract painting early learned to draw, to use perspective and color in painting representational pictures with skill. They mastered the specific techniques of their craft before they proceeded to a new or abstract type of painting. So, too, may mastery of specific instructional techniques be prerequisite to true artistry in teaching.

What is the current state of the art and science of educating teachers in this country? The storm of educational criticism after World War II, which first struck the schools, is now breaking over the colleges. It first hit teacher education, but is rapidly spreading to other areas of higher education. The sharpest critics of teacher education maintain that conditions are deplorable, and even those within the establishment admit that all is not well. We simply are not doing as well as we know and as well as we must do. Phi Delta Kappa is to be congratulated upon calling this conference, whose purpose is to stimulate constructive action.

However critical we may be today of teacher education in this country, we should recognize that, viewed from an historical and international perspective, it deserves much higher commendation than it typically receives. Historically, the record of the last twenty-five years is impressive, as the publication of *Milestones* in 1964 by the National Commission on Teacher Education and Professional Standards of the National Education Association documents. During this time, the number of teachers in American classrooms with a college degree rose from 50 to 90 per cent. With this increase in the quantity, and, we trust, in the quality of general education and subject matter specialization, the amount and character of professional education and practice has also improved. In this same period, the number of teachers with emergency credentials has dropped and salaries and other working conditions have improved. Internationally, there are few countries which do not envy our achievements in teacher education. I have had opportunity in recent years to study teacher education in many countries in Latin America, Australasia, Africa, and Eastern and Western Europe. The length and quality of programs of teacher education in the United States is by comparison impressive. As a senior and mature scholar from a university in a highly developed country, who was returning my visit, said to me toward the conclusion of his sojourn in the United States, "You are doing in a professional manner here with resources and trained staff what we are still trying to do for the most part on an amateur basis." His institution and program was one of the most advanced I had visited.

MAJOR PROBLEM CATEGORIES

The problem of educating teachers, or as our friends from abroad are inclined to say, and I think perhaps a little more forcefully, the *formation* of teachers, may be discussed under three major headings: 1) The Criterion Problem, 2) The Selection Problem, and 3) The Training Problem.

THE CRITERION PROBLEM

By what standards are the teacher and the program of teacher education to be judegd to determine whether improvement takes place as changes are made?

Of attempts to define what is a good teacher there is no end, with poor results. Why? Part of the reason is that so little time has been given to a study of the phenomenon of teaching as it occurs in the natural setting. Disproportionate energy has been devoted to moralizing and speculating on what teaching should be, and relatively little on what it is. This emphasis is changing. In many places across the country researchers are at work, imaginatively obtaining good basic records of what is going on in classrooms: Smith in Illinois, Flanders in Michigan, Bellack and Schueler in New York, Taba in California, to cite only a few. This documentation, some by audio tape recording, some by trained observers with carefully worked out observation schedules, is making a significant contribution toward describing teaching and its effects. What the teacher says or does can now be linked to what ensues in pupil behavior. At Stanford, we have been at work obtaining more refined descriptions of classroom interaction and developing a set of criteria that defines the kind of behavior we aim to produce in teachers in order to obtain a particular kind of pupil behavior. We have chosen to call these behavioral criteria "technical skills of teaching," which I shall describe shortly. In all, promising inroads on the tough, old criterion problem appear as we move away from global ratings and toward assessment of specific objectives with more meaningful descriptions of teacher behavior and resulting pupil behavior.

37

Who should go into training? Who should be selected to teach in a particular school or system? What can be predicted about how well a particular applicant or beginner will turn out? These are important questions. Here too, until quite recently, progress in finding satisfactory answers has been disappointingly slow. Why?

Perhaps the most serious difficulty is that the supply of those desiring to enter teaching has been so low that little or no selection could possibly take place. This, coupled with the high teacher dropout rate, forced us into taking all comers into training. Fortunately, this situation is changing. As teaching and other kinds of work in schools become more attractive larger numbers choose to enter the profession. Recent figures record that almost 40 per cent of bachelor's degree graduates of American colleges are prepared to teach. This is the largest single percentage for any occupation. The number of National Merit Scholars expressing interest in teaching has risen sharply, according to recent reports. The statistics of our own teacher-training program at Stanford clearly reflect the trend.

Admission procedures in colleges have included grade point averages, intellectual aptitude test scores, written letters of recommendation, and interviews, none of which relate highly to subsequent teaching success. The schools have done slightly better by relying upon a probationary period. The selective efforts in neither the school nor college have been very good. More discriminatory and valid selection procedures are needed. At Stanford, through micro-teaching, a procedure which I shall describe shortly, a performance test of predictive value is emerging. Performance in micro-teaching, before training, can with fair accuracy sort out those who later encounter trouble in training. We are beginning to use this procedure to eliminate trainees during the early part of training. We are working with some schools in the use of micro-teaching in their initial screening. We shall compare it with more traditional procedures for predicting success on the job.

The major current question is: Do programs of teacher education make demonstrable differences in how teachers teach? The need for a liberal education with some specialization in the subject to be taught is widely accepted as a logical, self-evident proposition, *without scientific proof*. No one asks whether or not four more hours of American history necessarily produce a better history teacher. But professional education is asked to demonstrate beyond question the usefulness of each unit of work in, for example, educational psychology or methodology. Of the uniquely professional work, the practice segment has been judged by those who have been through the programs to be the most useful, and the theoretical parts of least value. We need better evaluation of all segments of teacher education, including liberal and specialized education.

The 1963 Columbus, Ohio, Conference of the National Commission on Teacher Education and Professional Standards illustrated and evaluated the widespread ferment in devising new training programs. I shall not here repeat that review. Among the chief features of change are extension and improvement in liberal education and in subject-matter preparation; expansion of practice; greater use of newer media; and more involvement of the teachers in the schools. Our new program at Stanford, which incorporates a number of these and additional features, exemplifies what colleges and universities across the country are developing. Our trainees and our colleagues in the schools say that the new programs are more effective than the older ones. We are gathering evidence to ascertain whether this be true. Encouraging preliminary evidence suggests that the answer is yes. The new training does make a measurable and significant difference in teacher and pupil behavior.

TWO BROAD APPROACHES TO THE PROBLEM

In making investigations in any of these three major problem categories, two broad approaches to the study of teaching and the training of teachers may be delineated, both of which are essential and need concurrent development.

The first is a clinical or case study approach which grows out of a Gestalt or field theory orientation. In this, an interdisciplinary team of specialists from the relevant disciplines in the behavioral sciences and the subject-matter disciplines, together with educationists, study the relationships of teachers and pupils in natural classroom settings, exploring the classroom in all its complexity with a multiplicity of techniques. This approach is exemplified by work at Stanford beginning in the 1940's and is described initially in published form in the volume *The Teacher-Pupil Relationship.*[1] A clinic, first for teachers, later for administrators, was the vehicle. The purpose of the work was threefold: a scientific aim, to obtain better data concerning the nature of teaching; a training function, to help teachers in the schools to improve their teaching; and an instruction function, to develop better clinical materials for use in preservice training programs. Each of these purposes reinforced and strengthened the other. An essential characteristic of the endeavor was that it kept in view the wholeness of teaching and learning in the normal classroom while also permitting a scientific scrutiny of specifics, always in the context of providing services to teachers. We were handicapped, however, in this earlier effort by the lack of technological aids and specific techniques for obtaining good classroom records.

This lack is now being remedied through a second broad approach, analytical and experimental in character. New technological media have aided indispensably in its development. The approach concentrates upon analyzing either through observation or tape recordings the ongoing interaction of teachers and pupils. The aim of these current studies is to isolate specific units of teaching and learning behavior in their interrelationship.

TEACHER EDUCATION AT STANFORD

At Stanford we are attempting to define a set of specific technical skills of teaching and to develop training procedures that will enable teachers to use these skills in the classroom and through a variety of experimental procedures to describe

_____
[1] R. N. Bush, *The Teacher-Pupil Relationship.* New York: Prentice Hall, 1954.

the effects produced in pupils. The context of this work may be noted in the diagrams (pp. 42, 43, 44) which depict the overall design and rationale of our teacher education program. Note the classification of teaching behavior into two large categories, professional decisions and technical skills.

Professional Decisions and Technical Skills

Technical skills are an array of specific instructional techniques and procedures which a teacher may develop and draw upon as he teaches in the classroom. His choice of which ones are appropriate in a given situation at a particular moment is a professional decision. In the process of making professional decisions he develops his unique style of teaching. Herein lies the artistry of his work. His unique style will be enhanced as the teacher acquires a full repertoire of technical skills which he can use well. This requires a clear and specific definition of technical skills, a large amount of practice in using them, and an opportunity in a classroom to exercise his professional judgment in selecting the right ones at a given time.

To provide these conditions has been the aim of the program which we have designed. Pre-teaching practice is provided in a micro-teaching clinic in a summer prior to immersion in a part-time year of internship. The entire program is saturated with supervisory and student feedback.

The technical skills are in a rough state of development and definition. The 1964 formulation listed the following nine technical skills:

1. *Establishing set.*

The term "set" refers to the establishment of cognitive rapport between pupils and teacher to obtain immediate involvement in the lesson. Experience indicates a direct relationship between the effectiveness in establishing set and effectiveness in the total lesson. If the teacher succeeds in creating a positive set, the likelihood of pupil involvement in the lesson will be enhanced. For example, one technique for inducing positive set is through the use of analogies that have characteristics similar

41

A DESIGN FOR TEACHER EDUCATION
(PLAN I)

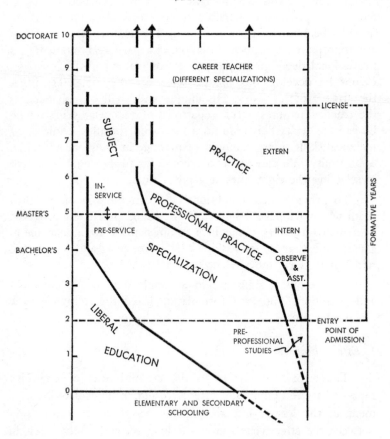

A DESIGN FOR TEACHER EDUCATION

(PLAN II)

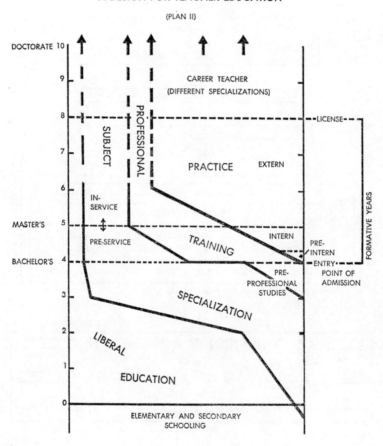

TEACHER EDUCATION AT STANFORD

```
┌─────────────────────────────────────────────┐
│               COMPETENCE                      │
│   AIM - PLAN - EXECUTION - EVALUATION         │
│        IN TEACHING AND LEARNING               │
└─────────────────────────────────────────────┘
                      ⬆
┌─────────────────────────────────────────────┐
│  PROFESSIONAL DECISIONS (WHEN TO DO WHAT)     │
└─────────────────────────────────────────────┘
                      ⬆
┌─────────────────────────────────────────────┐
│        TECHNICAL SKILLS   (HOW)               │
└─────────────────────────────────────────────┘
                      ⬆
```

·········· THE TRAINING PROGRAM ··········

·········· PRACTICE ··········

| MICRO TEACHING | CONTINUED STUDY IN THE TEACHING FIELD | HUMANISTIC AND SCIENTIFIC FOUNDATIONS METHODOLOGICAL, CURRICULAR & ADMINISTRATIVE PROBLEMS | CLINICAL EXERCISES |

·········· INTERNSHIP ··········

·········· BUILT AROUND THE PROBLEMS OF TEACHING ··········

```
                      ⬆
┌─────────────────────────────────────────────┐
│ ▭  CONCENTRATION IN A TEACHING FIELD  ▭       │
│                  and                          │
│ ▭  A SOLID BASE OF LIBERAL EDUCATION  ▭       │
│                                               │
│ ──  INTELLECTUAL AND PERSONAL EXCELLENCE  ──  │
└─────────────────────────────────────────────┘
```

to the concept, principle, or central theme of the lesson. By training interns in set induction procedures and having them apply these procedures in micro-teaching sessions, we can significantly improve subsequent classroom teaching.

2. *Establishing appropriate frames of reference.*

A student's understanding of the material of a lesson can be increased if it is organized and taught from several appropriate points of view. A single frame of reference provides a structure through which the student can gain an understanding of the materials. The use of several frames of reference deepens and broadens the general field of understanding more completely than is possible with only one. For example, the Emancipation Proclamation becomes more meaningful to the student when it is understood from the frames of reference of the Northern white abolitionist, the Southern white, the Negro slave in the seceded South, the free Negro, the European clothing manufacturer, the political leaders of England, and as an example of the reserved powers of the American President, than if it is simply discussed as the document issued by Lincoln which freed the slaves. Interns can be trained to become more powerful teachers as they are taught to identify many possible frames of reference that might be used in instruction, to make judicious selection from among them, and then to present them effectively.

3. *Achieving closure.*

Closure is complementary to set induction. Closure is attained when the major purposes, principles, and constructs of a lesson, or portion of a lesson, are judged to have been learned so that the student can relate new knowledge to past knowledge. It is more than a quick summary of the ground covered in a lesson. In addition to pulling together the major points and acting as a cognitive link between past knowledge and new knowledge, closure provides the pupil with a needed feeling of achievement. Closure is not limited to the completion of a lesson. It is also needed at specific points within the lesson so that pupils may know where they are and where they are going. Experience indicates that interns can be trained in this skill.

4. Using questions effectively.

The ability to ask provocative, answerable, and appropriate questions, and thus to involve pupils actively, is one of the critical skills in teaching. The micro-teaching clinic has proven to be an effective means for developing this skill. Novice teachers tend to ask questions which are either so general as to be vague and impossible to answer satisfactorily or so specific that they require a one-word, "fill-in" response, which tends to kill further responses. This conclusion is based upon observation and analysis of more than two hundred TV recordings of classroom lessons. Exercises for use in the micro-teaching clinic have been devised to build proficiency in preparing and using questions: factual, conceptual, thought-provoking, discussion-stimulating, heuristic questions. The procedure is, first, to instruct the intern in skillful questioning techniques and then to have him view video tape demonstrations of skillful practice. He then applies these techniques in micro-teaching sessions. Through supervisor and student feedback, and by viewing video tapes of his practice sessions, the intern is helped to correct faulty responses and to consolidate his effective practices.

5. Recognizing and obtaining attending behavior.

Interns can be trained to become more sensitive to the classroom behavior of pupils. The successful experienced teacher, through visual cues, quickly notes indications of interest or boredom, comprehension or bewilderment. Facial expressions, directions of the eyes, the tilt of the head, and bodily posture offer commonly recurrent cues which make it possible for the skilled teacher to evaluate his classroom performance according to the pupil's reactions. He can then change his "pace," vary the activity, introduce new instructional strategies as necessary, and improve the quality of his teaching. Unlike his more experienced counterpart, the intern teacher has difficulty in perceiving and interpreting these visual cues. Through 16mm motion picture films, and 35mm still picture protocols of classrooms, and video tape recordings of interns in micro-teaching sessions, supervisors are able to sensitize interns to visual cues of pupils' attending and non-attending behavior.

6. *Control of participation.*

Micro-teaching sessions enable interns to analyze the kinds of pupil-teacher interaction which characterize their teaching. Control of pupils' participation is one important variable in successful learning for pupils. Micro-teaching sessions provide an opportunity for interns to practice different techniques for encouraging or discouraging classroom interaction and to gain insight into the causal relationship between a series of teacher-pupil interactions. When an intern develops the skill to analyze and to control the use of his accepting and rejecting remarks, his positive and negative reactions, his patterns of reward and punishment, he has taken a major step toward effective teaching.

7. *Providing feedback.*

The feedback process in the training of teachers may be simply stated as providing "knowledge of results." Interns often ignore the availability of information accessible during the lesson. Questioning, visual cues, informal examination of performance, are immediate sources of feedback. Interns can be taught appropriate techniques to elicit feedback from students and to modify their lesson accordingly. Teachers unconsciously tap a variety of feedback sources, but unless they are sensitized they tend to rely unevenly on a limited number of students as "indicators" and to rely on a restricted range of feedback cues.

8. *Employing rewards and punishments (reinforcement).*

Reinforcing desired pupil behavior through the use of reward and punishment is an integral part of the teacher's role as director of classroom learning. Substantial psychological evidence confirms the value of reinforcement in the learning process. The acquisition of knowledge of specific techniques of reward and punishment and the development of skill in using them appropriately in specific situations is most important in training a beginning teacher. Experience indicates that interns can acquire skill through micro-teaching practice in reinforcement of pupil learning.

9. *Setting a model.*

The importance of analyzing and imitating model behavior is a basic assumption supporting the use of observation in a training program. Because of the brief, simple character of the micro-teaching situation, it is possible to provide good models of specific technical skills as an integral part of training. Models can be brief and relatively focused, hence more easily analyzed and imitated. Two levels of skill can be identified: the ability to analyze behavior and the ability to imitate it successfully. The hypothesis, as yet untested, is that interns can be trained to improve their ability to analyze and imitate teaching models. Such skills, it is reasoned, will open a wider range of alternatives and provide for more effective self-perception.

For use in the summer of 1965, the list of technical skills was reformulated in the spring under five major headings as follows:

1. *Initiating behaviors*

   a) directing the task
   b) establishing set
   c) formulating behavioral objectives
   d) diagnosing learning

2. *Presenting (communicating) behaviors*

   a) discussing
   b) lecturing
   c) using questioning techniques
   d) pacing the lesson
   e) establishing frames of reference
   f) distinguishing between concepts and illustrations, and using them

3. *Consolidating behaviors*

   a) reviewing
   b) achieving closure
   c) using repetition

4. *Monitoring behaviors*

   a) controlling participation
   b) obtaining attending behavior
   c) using rewards and punishments

5. *Evaluating behaviors*

   a) combining grades
   b) diagnosing a specific learning difficulty

By the time this material is published, the list and the groupings will have changed, as we are, it must be emphasized, just at the beginning in our exploration of the subject.

Illustrations of Specific Training Activities

The specific ways in which we have been attempting to develop these teaching skills in our program include:
1. Micro-teaching
2. 35mm time-lapse photography
3. Clinical exercises
4. Technical skill performance levels
5. Video tape recording of classrooms in the schools
6. Vignettes of teaching
7. Supervisory training in the schools

1. *Micro-teaching*

Micro-teaching is a scaled-down teaching exercise which has been developed at Stanford to serve two purposes:

   a) to provide practice in teaching prior to the assumption of responsibility in the classroom, and
   b) to permit research on training effects under controlled conditions.

It is a procedure whereby a trainee teaches a brief lesson (five to ten minutes) in his teaching subject field to a small group of pupils (up to five). Typically, these brief lessons are video tape recorded and immediately played back so that the trainee may see how he has taught. He also receives information on how the students and one or more supervisors judge his teaching, on

49

scales specifically prepared for this purpose. The lesson is critiqued, specific suggestions for improvement are developed, and the lesson is then re-taught to another group of pupils, with results noted. This is illustrated in brief video tape record sequence which can be viewed at the Stanford Teacher Education Program office.

The micro-teaching clinic was held in 1965 in eight classrooms on Stanford's inner Quadrangle. Of these eight, four contained video tape units, a picture of which may be seen on page 57. These are portable video tape recorders and monitors which make possible a visual and audio tape of the teaching performance, the tapes being immediately available for replay by trained technicians for use as a stimulus in supervisory conference, and for repeated use in later research.

Micro-teaching students were recruited from local high schools and trained for six hours in the use of the Stanford Teacher Competence Appraisal Guide, copies of which are available from the Stanford Teacher Education Program office. The students are paid for their participation during the summer. One major advantage of this arrangement is that selection and control can be exercised to obtain students who meet specified requirements such as age, sex, intellectual and achievement levels, social, economic, and racial background.

Following is a description of the form the micro-teaching clinic assumed in the summer of 1965, after two years' trial. On the first day, each trainee taught a five minute diagnostic lesson to a group of five students. The purpose was to obtain an evaluative record of the intern's beginning performance and to begin to familiarize him with the video tape and supervisory system. Evaluations were made of the interns' performances by the students and a Stanford supervisor. Following this, each intern was scheduled in the clinic in two four-stage teach/reteach cycles each week for a period of three weeks. At the beginning of the cycle each week, the intern received one hour of instruction in a specific technical skill selected for emphasis during that week. He then entered a four-stage teach/re-teach sequence: 1) Intern taught a five-minute lesson to a small group of students and was observed by a Stanford supervisor. 2) Immediately following, he participated in a five-minute supervisory conference.

3) He then, after a few minutes' interval, taught another five-minute lesson to a new team of students being observed by the same Stanford supervisor. 4) This was followed at once by another supervisory conference. These cycles proceed independently of video tape recordings. However, in the summer of 1965, every other one of these four-stage teach/reteach cycles was video tape recorded. This teach/re-teach cycle occupied four days each week. The fifth day was devoted to special attention to the individual needs of each intern.

At the end of the first three weeks, the micro-teaching clinic took a one-week break. At this time the trainees had a week of rest, plus some instruction in techniques of classroom discipline. They were also organized into teams in their respective subject areas in preparation for the micro-teaching class, the form which the clinic took during the fifth, sixth, and seventh weeks. During this fourth week the staff prepared the way for the program of the last three weeks of the summer. This included a) planning for the micro-teaching classes during the fifth, sixth, and seventh weeks; b) the beginning of a tutor program for the trainees, an integral part of micro-teaching, which consisted of having each intern tutor a local high school student who was in need of some remedial work for a three-week period; and c) the development of an observation program for the interns to visit local summer high school classes.

The format during the fifth, sixth, and seventh weeks consisted of groups of interns, ranging in number from two to five. Each team prepared a twelve-day teaching unit under the direction of its special subject supervisor. This was taught to a micro-class of students who remained together as a group for the twelve days. Lessons were of twenty minutes' duration and were observed by those of the intern team not teaching that day, as well as by the supervisor. Each lesson was followed immediately by a twenty-minute supervisory conference in which the other interns also participated. Each day, the students evaluated the teaching, and at the end of the unit the trainees evaluated the students' learning. The purpose of the twelve-day micro-class was to give the interns an opportunity to plan and to teach a unit in their subject and to approach a little more closely the complexity of a normal teaching situation. The interns devised

51

and used evaluative instruments to find how well the students had learned the materials presented. It gave them opportunity to teach longer lessons than in the beginning, to have a longer critique not only with supervisors but with peers participating. The sessions were video taped every other day so that this record was available in addition to the other forms of feedback.

The criterion measure used during the micro-teaching clinic was the Stanford Teacher Competence Appraisal Guide, which was completed by the students and by the supervisors. This guide consists of thirteen items of seven-interval forced choice scales biased toward superior ratings to eliminate J-curve effects. The guide, now in the second year of use in its present form, grows out of more than a decade of experimentation and revision. The present thirteen semi-independent items were constructed from the results of a factor analysis on an earlier guide composed of twenty-four items. The guide has demonstrated adequate reliability on its specific items and limited evidence suggests that scores on it are related to student test performance.

A preliminary scanning of the results of experimentation and other forms of evaluation in 1965 confirms directions delineated in 1963 and 1964. Trainees continue strongly to support the program. Interns showed significant gains on nine of the twelve items in the appraisal guide over the summer quarter. Performance in micro-teaching predicts subsequent classroom performance, especially at the two ends of the spectrum, the stars and the problems. Trainees who receive student feedback, view video tape recordings of their teaching, and who have supervisory criticism all gain significantly more than do those who do not.

Further experimentation is pushing into new territory. For example, in some of the studies under the immediate supervision of McDonald and Allen,[1] in the summer of 1965, which focused upon reinforcing certain teacher behaviors and providing models,

---

[1] See the following unpublished mimeographed statements prepared in 1965 for the School of Education, Stanford University, by Frederick J. McDonald, Dwight W. Allen, and Michael E. J. Orme: "The Effects of Self-Feedback and Reinforcement on the Acquisition of a Teaching Skill"; "Effects of Feedback and Practice Conditions on the Acquisition of a Teaching Strategy"; and "The Effects of Modeling and Feedback Variables on the Acquisition of a Complex Teaching Strategy."

noticeable training effects show up: Teachers can be trained to reinforce student behavior and noticeably to increase student participation and to use questioning techniques so as to cause pupils to elaborate their answers. The experiments show also which combination of feedback procedures is most powerful. Another type of experiment, immediately supervised by Fortune, Gage, and Shutes,[2] attempted to delineate explaining behavior in teachers and to determine if this capacity has some consistency over different groups of pupils and topics. Results at first reading suggests that in this instance it is consistent for different groups of students, but not for different topics.

2. 35mm time-lapse photography in studying attending behavior.

One of the technical skills selected as of potential importance is labeled "attending behavior," in commonsense language: "Are students paying attention?" Stated more precisely, it refers to the extent to which a student appears to direct his attention to the same point of interest as the majority of his class peers, which is presumed to be related to the learning task placed before the class by the teacher. The first step was to determine if attending behavior could be identified and reliably measured. To accomplish this, two raters were placed at the rear of a classroom and both continuously rated the attending behavior of each student, taking about one and one-half minutes to rate each person in the entire class, the process then being repeated for the entire class period. The camera was placed between the raters and a picture of the class was taken every one and one-half minutes. Substantially, the camera recorded what the raters observed. This photographic record was then rated at the university by a different pair of raters. Inter-rater agreement betweeen the live and the photographic observations, based on forty-five observations in forty-five classrooms, was .65. The high inter-rater agreement may be explained by the fact that the attending behavior of any one student was always seen against the background of the at-

[2]J. C. Fortune, N. L. Gage, and R. E. Shutes, "Generality of Ability to Explain." Paper presented at meetings of the American Educational Research Association, Chicago, February, 1966. Stanford University, School of Education.

tending behavior of the entire class. Earlier research that used photography for recording behavior in classrooms used pictures of a single individual or just a few individuals and then attempted to record, quantitatively, changes in facial expressions, body postures, eye blinks, hand movements. The recording process now established, however, provides a clear record of most students in the classroom. When the expected behavior in the classroom under investigation is known, for example—whether the teacher is lecturing, conducting a discussion, or giving a demonstration—the investigator can determine in each picture the modal orientation of the class toward that task and can more readily detect who deviates. These data can be used in a variety of ways both for training and research. For example, a single student's attending behavior can be followed over periods of time. By having teachers watch these records of classroom attending behavior, it is possible to sensitize them to many of the cues in attending behavior, thus giving a teacher feedback which he can use in evaluating the quality of the teaching and the degree of achievement experienced by the learner. This is not to suggest that attending behavior alone is a sufficient requirement for effective teaching-learning situations. Where attending behavior is low, however, it may be speculated that little learning takes place. In studies by McGraw[3] in 1964 at Stanford, using time-lapse photography with two groups of trainees and providing them with photographic feedback and supervisory discussion, significant gains were recorded in controlling and improving the amount of attending behavior over a control group which did not have the benefit of the training procedure. Several relationships that have been discovered support the proposition that attending behavior relates to learning: Attending behavior is dependent upon IQ and grades; IQ is independent of attending behavior and grades; grades are dependent upon IQ and attending behavior. Another way in which these records have been used is to plot the mean of attending behavior in a trainee's class over a period of time. This feedback is designed to alert the trainee to periods when his class is generally not attentive.

[3]Frank McGraw, "The Use of 35mm. Time-lapse Photography on a Feedback and Observation Instrument in Teacher Education." Unpublished doctoral dissertation, Stanford University, October, 1965.

The mean attending behavior in all classes plotted showed low attending behavior during the first and fourth quarters of the class period, with the attending behavior rising during the second and third quarters. This raises interesting questions about classroom strategies that might raise attending behavior at the beginning and at the end of the class period. Interns were encouraged to plan activities which would raise the level of attending behavior during low periods. This has proved to be possible. Initial results appear sufficiently promising to suggest that we are just at the beginning in the use of 35mm time-lapse photography in the study of teaching.

The equipment used is relatively simple and inexpensive, in comparison with other kinds of classroom recording, especially video tape records. The record can be quickly made without great expense. Details of equipment are available in a technical report.

3. *Clinical exercises.*

A type of instruction, with related materials, developing only slowly thus far but with potential, is the "clinical exercise." One of these, entitled "Diagnosing and Treating a Learning Difficulty," will illustrate the procedure. Each trainee selects two students from one of the classes in which he is serving as an intern teacher, one with whom he has a high degree of rapport and one with whom he senses low rapport, and both of whom are achieving below measured ability and/or previous performance. The intern systematically analyzes the pupils' learning difficulties, selects one aspect, and proposes a specific treatment. A program of remediation is planned and carried out over the necessary days or weeks. Measures are devised and administered to assess pupil gains. Typically, the difficulty is at least partially remedied, and the level of rapport with the student originally rejected is raised significantly. We intend to develop, and to test at Stanford and in other institutions, a number of such clinical exercises. The unique advantage of such exercises is that they aim to present theoretical background, to relate it to technical skills, and to provide practice and follow-through to determine how well the trainee can apply such skills in the classroom.

4. *Technical skill performance levels.*

Currently, we are attempting to establish teaching performance levels in selected technical skills and other classroom operations so that the trainee may request observation and video tape recording when he considers that he can perform at a satisfactory level. He proceeds, during the year, to tackle as rapidly as possible all of the skills and operations on which he must demonstrate a satisfactory level of performance. When he has completed this, part of his internship evaluation will be based on the level of performance he has reached. These "performance criteria" are being adapted for each subject-matter field.

5. *Video tape recording in classrooms in the schools.*

After the intern has, in the summer, experienced some teaching, and has come to expect that he will be observed, video tape recorded, and critiqued, he moves out into the schools, where as an intern under supervision he assumes full responsibility to teach one or two classes for the entire year. The video tape units used in the summer (see page 57) are portable. One operator can transport and set them up in school classrooms during the passing time between periods. This makes possible a program of video tape recording of the intern's regular teaching in the schools, a logical continuation and extension of the training in the summer. Tapes are made throughout the entire year as training and experimentation require. These tapes are available for the trainee and his school and university supervisor and for those who are teaching the theoretical work at the university. Clips of these tapes thus become a part of the clinical material for instructional purposes in the training program.

The video tape recording in the school takes place with almost no noticeable interruption of the normal classroom setting, no special lighting or other "props." This has become possible not only because of the technical quality of the equipment but also because of the experience and familiarity with the procedure by the interns, administrators, and teachers in the schools, and because of the care exercised by a sensitive and sensible group of video tape operators who initially were teachers. An arrangement such as this has distinct advantages over more elaborate studio-type television recording, which limits investigation to a few fitted classrooms and expensive, complex monitoring studios and mobile units.

6. *Vignettes of teaching.*

The use of models of excellence in training teachers, both in the performance of technical skills and making good professional decisions, needs to be more fully explored. We have made a modest beginning with a series of short (2- to 4-minute) film clips, in which experienced teachers, who also supervise

Portable video tape unit used in
Stanford micro-teaching

interns, teach lessons to micro-teaching students. The aim is to demonstrate alternative ways of dealing with specific classroom situations. The first set of films is on skill in establishing classroom control, which poses special problems for beginning teachers. These brief films were only partly scripted, being pre-structured to the extent that the situation was described, both to students and to the teacher, and then allowed to develop naturally within the limitations imposed by pre-planned specifications of the type of teaching strategy or maneuver that was to be attempted to cope with the specified kind of problem. On the basis of limited use of this material with interns, the effort seems to be worth further exploration. The trainees report that the films provide them with considerable insight into the nature of the problem of classroom control and that they have been stimulated to try to use and adapt some of the approaches illustrated. One important aim in this first group of films is to illustrate a variety of ways of coping with similar problems, to show the importance of individuality of style in the use of any procedure. It is difficult for beginners to grasp that there are many different ways of performing a particular skill with effectiveness. They are groping so hard for *an* answer that they are likely to feel that there must be *one* right answer. These films may also be helpful to supervisors and trainees in their discussion of a particular skill, and of alternative consequences of using particular styles and strategies in coping with a specific kind of classroom problem.

This incursion into filming models of excellence is thus far so limited as scarcely to warrant mention. It needs bold exploration. We need many video recordings of a few acknowledged masters who are at the pinnacle of excellence in teaching in this country and abroad. To foster an understanding of the true artistry of teaching, these models need to be used widely, not alone for detailed study of technical skills but also to demonstrate how a whole teaching performance is put together, how professional decisions are made.

We need to break the limitations of some current thinking which employs only reinforcement in the process of shaping or molding behavior. There is room for excellent models, and the contemplation of these by the trainee himself, where he enters more actively into the growth process instead of being treated as a simple piece of protoplasm to be shaped.

7. *Supervisory training.*

We now are beginning to develop the use of video tape recordings of micro-teaching and intern teaching in the normal classroom settings in a program for training both school and university supervisors. Recordings of teacher-pupil interaction prove stimulating to groups of supervisors as they study how to improve their skills in supervision. Groups of supervisors with a training leader find it advantageous to have a tape which they can view, stopping it where necessary to discuss, and even to replay. They discover where and why agreements and disagreements occur, observe the effect of specific suggestions on training, and speculate on more effective alternative. This brings a reality heretofore lacking into supervisory training.

This concludes the examples which have been selected from the Stanford program but which only serve to illustrate what is taking place in teacher education programs that are designed to encourage experimentation and other types of research and development concurrently with training. The program illustrated lies at the heart of the new Center for Research and Development in Teaching which has been established at Stanford under a grant from the U. S. Office of Education.

CONCLUSION

I return in conclusion to refer to the two broad approaches to the study of teaching and the conduct of teacher education referred to in the beginning: 1) the clinical, intuitive, artistic, and humanistic; and 2) the experimental, analytical, objective, and scientific. The bulk of what I have presented and the illustrations which I have drawn from the program at Stanford, which could be as well or better illustrated with different examples from elsewhere, suggests how strongly the tide runs in the scientific direction in teacher education today. This is the current fashion and emphasis, long overdue and much needed, which I heartily favor. I support and encourage it—even try to understand, participate in, and contribute to it when I can. But I must call at this time for an equally bold thrust on the humanistic and artistic frontier, which needs bolstering and improving, and which is just as important. Both approaches need, in my judgment, to take place simultaneously in the same setting so that they may interpenetrate and draw upon, reinforce, and correct each other. Each approach by itself has limitations which tend to disappear and to turn into strengths when they are pursued together. Promising features which characterize both approaches today are that they center upon teacher-pupil and teacher-group interaction, in both scaled-down and natural class settings. They both prosper most when experienced teachers and administrators in the schools collaborate closely with those who are working in the teacher education institutions, and when specialists from the various behavioral sciences work closely with the educationists. Under these circumstances, the possibility is enhanced for the formation of a fully developed teacher who possesses a high degree of skill in technical matters and the wisdom to use good professional judgment in employing a wide range of these skills. Such a rationale should underlie our new programs for educating teachers.

We are beginning in this country to obtain agreement on the major elements that should be included in a sound program of teacher education: a broad liberal education, specialization in the subject matters to be taught, professional training, and controlled and supervised practice. We suffer, however, from too great diversity in how these are put together into a program in different institutions. For example, the variability in length of training programs is much too great, ranging as it does from one to eight years. The duration has probably been too long in some instances and too short in others. What is called a program is too often only a haphazardly thrown-together bundle of truncated expediencies. Unfortunately, this seems almost to be what some critics of teacher education want us to retrogress to. But consensus along more constructive lines appears to be emerging. We are almost at the point of being able to agree upon a period of training that is sufficiently long, rigorous, and relevant to enable trainees for all levels and subjects to develop a competence required for effective teaching. California recently took such a step in bringing the requirements for all levels of beginning teaching up to the M.A. degree. A planned program of teacher education does not mean a few weeks in a summer school, a little frosting on the undergraduate cake, or arrangements whereby, as one critic with whom I recently discussed the matter concluded, "anyone with drive can complete the courses needed for credentials in his spare time." It does mean some consolidation into a few broad patterns which we might agree upon and within which we might work in our various institutions. The Stanford program is an example of one of the types of patterns that might be considered. (See diagram on page 44.) Here the commitment to teaching comes late, with a year or two of post-baccalaureate work tied closely to a few initial years of continued training in the schools. Internship programs developing over the past decade have been in the direction of this pattern. Another broad pattern within which we might operate would be one that is equally long and rigorous but begins in the undergraduate years. I mapped out the broad outline of a program of this type earlier this year in a proposed new design for teacher education at the June meeting of the National TEPS Conference in New York. It is depicted in the two diagrams on pages 42 and 43.

The ingredients are the same in these two major designs, you will note, and the general principles are similar. The chief difference is the point of admission, which occurs two years earlier in one than in the other. However, in both patterns the four basic elements of liberal education, specialization, professional training, and practice are merged and continue with gradual induction into full practice, with licensure taking place only after competence, as judged by professional colleagues in schools and universities, has been proven in the field.

If we could have widespread experimentation in educating teachers within two or perhaps three such frameworks, I think that we could rapidly strengthen teacher training programs in this country. I doubt the wisdom of trying to compare the relative effectiveness of one of these approaches with another. Time would be more profitably spent in seeing how well objectives were being met within each of these frameworks. One chief reason that advance in research in teacher education has not been greater is the lack of clearly delineated, well-organized programs with basic rationales, clearly defined objectives, some internal discipline, and a steady progression of trainees through them. With carefully planned, coherent, and integrated designs, better research and experimentation on the relative effectiveness of a variety of training procedures becomes possible. This was the objective that compelled us to adopt a new program at Stanford. If we evaluate well within each of several patterns, and make modifications accordingly, I would not be concerned whether one pattern moves closer to another. There may be several distinctive patterns, each of which accomplishes its objectives. The goal is to achieve programs of excellence that reach their objectives.

Discussion of the Bush Paper

MORK: To the careful reader it is clear that Mr. Bush basically recognizes three fundamental considerations in his paper: 1) the press of teachers to become truly professional and the corresponding press on teacher education in the same direction; that is, to discover and develop a truly professional education for teachers; 2) the reciprocal components of art and science in the worth of the effective teacher; and 3) the fact that teachers can be taught to be more effective by a masterful blending of that art and science in their own teaching behavior.

The most exciting emphasis throughout his discerning paper is upon good teaching as the effective use of a number of identifiable skills. Building upon an insightful analysis of teaching-learning processes and also on the research studies of classroom behavior which are now beginning to pile up, he identifies several such technical skills for special attention and description.

Our contributor does not make the mistake of denying that art does play an important role in the performance of the highly successful teacher. Indeed, he underlines the basic importance of skills as the foundation tools upon which the artful teacher develops his unique style, and his artistry, as he exercises his professional judgment in classroom situations. Even so does a great violinist master the skills of performance before he presumes to reach full expression as a performing virtuoso!

I would hope that teacher educators, concerned with the professional practice dimension in teacher preparation, will study very carefully the nine technical skills which Mr. Bush first identifies. It may well be that some teacher educators will wish to classify technical skills somewhat differently and come up with a slightly different list, even as Bush moved on to five major headings. I hope, however, that all will seek a list of clearly identifiable behaviors which they will then seek to teach as skills to their future teachers.

This development of a repertoire of basic competencies could well be probed with each student teacher by such questions as:

Can you establish a cognitive set as a basis for pupil involvement in a lesson?

Very well, demonstrate this.

or:

Can you ask a factual question (or a conceptual question, or a discussion-stimulating question)?

Very well, demonstrate!

or:

Can you use reinforcement of pupil responses in such a manner that pupil activity and participation are increased

Again: demonstrate!

The list can continue through a whole series of skills deemed important to that particular student-teacher at that level, with those pupils, and in that field.

As Bush notes later in his paper, each trainee proceeds during the year to tackle as rapidly as possible all the list of skills and operations on which he must demonstrate a satisfactory level of performance.

He adds that

internship evaluation will be based on the level of performance which he has reached.

This approach clearly moves teaching from the realm of the mystical or mysterious, or from a vague holistic approach, to a combination of activities and procedures which are closely related to teaching objectives, which possess greater clarity and definition, and which have operational and behavior identification. From here, of course, we can move to an analysis of which kinds of behaviors are appropriate to the achievement of specific instructional objectives, be they in the cognitive, affective, or skill areas, or at the appropriate levels of pupil characteristics. As our contributor notes, "These are being uniquely built for each subject-matter field."

This approach can also provide us with the reply to that disconcerting challenge which, as Bush notes, is thrown at teacher educators, "to demonstrate beyond question the usefulness of each unit of work in educational psychology or methodology," something which has never been asked of any other preparatory program for any of the other professions.

But let us accept this challenge, too. After all, education *is* our business, and we should rightly be the ones who investigate the educative process wherever it is found.

The paper we have just heard identifies other aspects of the professional education problem. It emphasizes the rapid growth of empirical and experimental data in the area of classroom behavior. As it says, referring to the earlier case-study approach period, "We were handicapped . . . by lack of technological aids and specific techniques for obtaining . . . [such classroom] data." But this is indeed being remedied on a number of fronts and we would hope that one of the outcomes of this Phi Delta Kappa symposium will be added stimulation to an even greater effort in this area.

On my own campus, for example, some of us have been working for the past three years on the identification of teacher and pupil classroom verbal behavior in terms of Bloom's well known taxonomy.

We also need much careful research on the pupil learnings which are associated with greater or lesser effectiveness in the use of certain of the behaviors and skills cited. Similarly, we need more intensive study of the personality characteristics of the future teachers who are able to learn certain of these techniques with greater or lesser readiness.

Here again, if this symposium stimulates greater effort, Phi Delta Kappa will have contributed richly to the achievement of one of its major goals, the expansion of research for the improvement of our profession.

As one responsible for a student teaching program, I am particularly excited about the greatly improved evaluation of student-teacher growth which is made possible by a better identification of skills and behaviors which can be considered as the objectives of a student-teaching experience. Too often this evaluation has been vague and global, and so shot through with halo effect that many colleges have surrendered weakly to the temptation to simply pass everyone in student teaching with no attempt to ascertain growth in separate identifiable competencies.

Mr. Bush also highlights the advances in technology which have enabled us now to capture classroom events for later study and analysis—the time-lapse photography, and the audio- and video-tapes, for example.

We could also mention that programed learning is forcing us to be much more analytical about the step-by-step procedures involved in developing concepts or skills. This, too, will help (and force) us to be more discerning and to move from the vague and haloistic to the well-directed and well-considered.

I am not going to dwell on Mr. Bush's description of the micro-teaching developed at Stanford. This highly ingenious procedure speaks for itself and should be studied by us all, emulated, adapted, and given continuous intensive research and study. To me it poses the challenge to test the growth of student teachers under such a program and to compare the development of their skills with those developed by others who are simply allowed to grow like Topsy, albeit with some help in planning instruction and in learning how to adjust to children or youth.

Certainly we all have a responsibility, in colleges and public schools alike, to acquaint ourselves very thoroughly with these developments for increasing the effectiveness of our supervisory skills in analyzing and evaluating teaching. We will hear more, of course, of the public schools' stake in this process tomorrow morning.

Before I close, let us remind ourselves (and I am sure that Professor Bush agrees) that the development of a highly skilled classroom technician is not all there is to the development of a truly professional teacher. It is indeed another of these necessary but not sufficient conditions. In giving emphasis, however, to the technical skills, we *have* broken through the mystique to a much clearer view of some of teacher education's most important dimensions.

DAVIES: I'd be interested, in light of the discussion of Mr. Broudy's comments, to know enough more about the role of foundations, or whatever you call them here, in the program that you describe.

BUSH: We feel that the three major components of the professional side of the training program, in addition to the practice, are the foundational fields, the curriculum and methodological part relating to the specific subject, and a general field which we call secondary education: administration, guidance, and other general considerations in the management of the schools. All three of these are important components. The foundational part of the program as organized at the moment begins with psychological foundations, moves to the sociological, and then to the historical, and philosophical toward the end. The foundations, the curriculum, and methodological parts parallel the practice. We are in the process of finding ways in which the foundational work can be taught, using clinical materials to make it as relevant as possible. Mr. McDonald, Mr. Thomas, and others who teach foundational work in the program are here and may want to respond specifically. We see it as most important, and we're trying (this is really back of the question which I raised this morning with Mr. Broudy) to see how this material can be made more relevant by having it offered along with the practice, and by using materials from the practice, within a common framework of behavioral objectives. The important and difficult part is application. We certainly haven't solved it. Perhaps some of my colleagues wish to comment.

McDONALD: You might tell them a few of the things we do to interrelate this. I worked with Dwight Allen in helping to plan some of the micro-teaching sections and I teach the educational psychology course at the same time they're in micro-teaching. One of the first things I have students do is study Bloom's taxonomy of objectives. They also get emphasis on how to write objectives for programs of instruction. This is a training function that I monitor so student teachers can plan their micro-teaching lessons in the light of specific objectives. Also, the kind of psychology of learning that I'm teaching in the summer presumably is relevant to some of the things that they do in the teaching of lessons, though we don't have the coordination worked out perfectly. What we do is continually exchange ideas so that I can comment on the problems they have and in turn give them ideas for things they might try out in the micro-teaching. This is the way that I work. Eventually I would expect to use many of the tapes that are taken both from regular classrooms and in the micro-teaching as the basis for discussion of certain psychological principles.

COGAN: The title of the talk this afternoon was "The Science and Art of Educating Teachers." Mr. Bush, you yourself said you were largely preoccupied with the *science* of teaching. Could I suggest that it might be fruitful for us to become occupied with the scientific investigation of artistic teaching? Let me give an example. Whenever we talk to naive graduate students or undergraduates about their great teachers, their best teachers, we're almost certain to find them expressing a preference for the inspirational teacher, the teacher who captured them, the charismatic teacher. If you observe their behavior in those teachers' classes, you note that they pay attention, they read, they study; there are a lot of outcomes that are obviously good. But if I press a little further and say, "Let's take a look at some of the *other* outcomes of this kind of great artistic teaching," I occasionally find some very disturbing things. For example, sometimes one of the outcomes seems to be that the students learn dependence; that is, they become dependent upon the charismatic teacher, or the great teacher, for their ideas. They become disciples. This is a suppression of creativity, and I have noticed this especially in the graduate students of some of the "greatest" of our collegiate instructors. I just wonder whether it wouldn't pay us *not* simply to put value on artistic teaching and leave this value undefined but rather to take a close look at artistic teaching and perhaps to press it until we are able to specify a little better some of the outcomes. I'm not talking solely about negative outcomes. I simply talked about these negative outcomes to make the case that artistic teaching needs examination too.

BUSH: I couldn't agree more with the proposition that we ought to get the models of excellence as people suggest them.

We ought to subject them to careful scrutiny. I don't know whether we'll find all the negative things you suggest in them, but I do think we ought to study them. One of the quivering chunks of deathless prose which I couldn't include because we lacked time today was a strong plea to add the study of biography, autobiography, and other literature about the great teachers in all eras throughout history. We suffer from too little of this. I think that the humanistic side, Mr. Broudy, of the history of education could be very much enlivened. Recently, I have been reading of the way in which John Stuart Mills's father taught his son, and I'm re-reading material (not the badly excerpted paperback books of readings but the sources) from *Emile* and *The Confessions* of Rousseau, who is somewhat out of favor at the moment. I think we and our trainees might well look back at material of this type, study it carefully and, as we move into a period when the machines may be able to take over much routine in teaching, we may be able to approximate conditions where the teacher can more nearly become a tutor, as prevailed in many instances in the past. These excellent examples may give important clues on such critical problems as, for example, motivation. I heartily concur in what you say, Mr. Cogan. We ought to study these examples carefully. We may find that all is not well in them, but our own horizons would be markedly broadened.

BOYAN: I would like to try to relate this last set of points to one point that Mr. Cogan made which could easily get lost in the shuffle of our discussion. The Stanford program unabashedly lays out certain behaviors toward which it is attempting to shape the behavior of interns. The Stanford Appraisal Guide has thirteen performance areas. Within each of those areas we are getting a little closer look at things like set, etc. One of the questions that remains relatively unanswered is what difference it makes when you shape that behavior. There is an underlying assumption that the model of behavior which has been invented does produce certain kinds of effects in pupils, in learners, and that this area itself is subject to scientific investigation. Yet the connection between the two is an assumed one, at least at this stage of the game. There are people who are working with us, and I am sure in other places, who have asked this question and hope to do something about it. Thus far, we really haven't made a great deal of progress when it comes to the notion of the "scientificness" of teaching or preparation of teachers in relating the criterion variables toward which we are pointing our efforts to the criterion variables which are associated with the behavior of youngsters.

BELLACK: Building on this notion of teaching as an art form, there is one frequently expressed point of view I think we might want to discuss. That is, if one conceives of teaching as an art form, then possibly when it comes to analyzing it one might look to the model of art criticism, for example, instead of scientific inquiry. I would like to hear Mr. Broudy comment on this. Do you consider it a possibly fruitful approach to look toward the development of a form of criticism of teaching similar to art criticism or literary criticism?

MORK: Might I put in another point here? Mr. McDonald referred to the fact that he, too, has been using Bloom's taxonomy. I'm wondering if there aren't many things, Mr. Cogan, in the artistic teacher dimension that you speak of, that might not be identified with or associated with certain aspects of the affective dimension in that taxonomy, so that they could be identified in very much the same way that I think is done here very largely in the cognitive realm. We can explore the emotional dimension of this just the way we can explore the intellectual, I think.

SCHUELER: Might I speak to the problem of patterning your own teaching after a model? As you know, one fate of a disciple is never to be as good as the model. Usually he is a weak carbon copy. Then the disciples of the disciples are usually even weaker, the farther away you get from the initial source of inspiration. One of the great boons, it seems to me, in the use of this highly individualistic medium we call closed circuit television (it's a mass medium but we're changing it around) is that it permits the individual to see himself as others see him and to experience himself as others experience him. In the process of modeling your behavior after others you look toward them as *you* perceive them, but by introducing this dimension of seeing yourself as others perceive you, you can objectivize your own image and therefore it is possible to obviate the very great dangers of placing too much dependence on models. I think we all must recognize that the art of teaching is not in the last analysis reducible to formulas or, as mentioned before, to the technicians in the classroom all doing the same thing. Teaching styles do and should differ and should be compatible with the individual personality of the teacher. To some extent these can be changed, but they have to be directed to the optimum expression that is possible within the personality configuration of the person who is to be trained. Therefore the use of television experience as a method of guided self-appraisal has many interesting possibilities. It's not confined to teaching either. It's appropriate to acting or any kind of communicative art in which the individual can experience himself as others experience him. I think this is the great contribution that this medium can now make.

BROUDY: May I, before we get any further, introduce a small sour note? Not in what Mr. Bush said but in this whole notion of the artist teacher. Now by any definition of art, or artistic activity, it would be quite difficult to construe the act of teaching as an act of artistic creation unless one is speaking of an artisan or craftsman. The nearest analogue we can get, I suppose, is acting. If the teacher acts and takes on a role as in a drama, I suppose this would be artistic work. I think it's taken for granted in aesthetic theory that artistic activity (in the fine arts) works with images of one kind or another. It transforms these into an aesthetic object, not an article of use, not an article of skill, and not any product other than its own performance. Teachers, I take it, do not perform merely for the sake of performing. We can speak analogically about teaching as an artistic performance, meaning that it engenders enthusiasm and appreciation in the beholder. For example, one might say that Babe Ruth hitting a home run was an artistic performance because (a) it does very well what it's trying to do, and (b) it does engender a kind of admiration for the skill with which it is done. But not even his wildest fans regarded Babe Ruth as an artist and what he did as an artistic product.

Teaching is a practical activity with an end and a means and a product. Art (or fine art at least) is not a practical activity with a goal, a means, and a product. Therefore, the attempt to compare them, except for general metaphorical purposes, may have results that we don't anticipate.

COGAN: I really hoped we'd get to the point of discussing what the practical arts are, and without getting stuck on the question of the definition of art. What I wanted to say before, if I may return to the topic of models and the use of models in teaching, is this: You might be interested in the use of video-tape recorder and some ideas of B. F. Skinner on precisely this question. We were talking about the use of models, and Skinner made a suggestion that I find extremely intriguing. We have already done some work with it. He said, "As long as you have this video-tape machine, why don't you let the teacher use *himself* as a model. That is, not only to see himself as others see him but to see *himself*, to analyze his strengths and weaknesses." Skinner went on to suggest that teachers be reinforced as they moved toward the maximization of their strengths. The idea that a man may build his individual teaching style upon his own performance and the strengths in it seems to me to have some value.

BOYAN: I just wonder whether we might ask Dwight Allen and Fred McDonald to tell Mr. Cogan of our anticipations of Mr. Skinner in terms of experiments which have been going on?

ALLEN: In our experimentation we ask the teacher to view an outside model, modeling a desired set of behaviors. Then we ask the teacher to view his own behavior, on the theory that his own performance, as he viewed it, was a model. Those parts of the model which reflected the behavior that was consonant with the outside model's behavior would then be reflected. In fact, the excerpt of the film that you saw was the result of one and one-half hours of training using this procedure, where the intern first gave a five-minute presentation. Then, through the use of models, we sought to change his behavior by asking questions. We showed him a model in which about 25 to 30 questions were asked within a five-minute instructional period, to demonstrate to him exactly the kind of questions a good teacher asks. He then practiced this type of questioning by teaching another five minute lesson, and looked at his own behavior on video-tape with a supervisor who reinforced him when he asked questions. In addition, the negative instances where he ignored the opportunity to ask questions were also pointed out to him. These are the types of modeling experiments we have been doing here at Stanford.

BOYAN: I think it's also appropriate here for Mr. McDonald to comment on what we have found with respect to self-viewing versus guided viewing.

McDONALD: The self-viewing condition by itself was always the least effective of the conditions, even when students were programmed to watch certain things. What Skinner has yet to learn after all these years is that the world is not a big Skinner box and a student does not always emit the kind of responses that you want him to emit. It turns out to be very hard for the student to, first of all, criticize his own behavior. We get results only when we do have somebody there with him right from the very beginning reinforcing the desired responses. Our modeling conditions always turn out to be more effective than our reinforcement conditions, because viewing a model then elicits some of this behavior on the part of students, which in turn we can reinforce. So, as we say around here, the modeling procedure is very good for the acquisition phase, and the reinforcement procedure is very effective to maintain performance. But just watching the behavior alone is a weak condition. I myself kept hoping that it would be effective, because it's more economical, but of itself it is not effective with that particular condition.

COGAN: Yes. I think perhaps I misrepresented Skinner's comment. He didn't mean that the teacher would simply watch himself but that his performance would be analyzed and it would be his own performance that he would use as a model.

STONE: I'd like to comment and ask Mr. Bush to respond. I don't know whether this is in the area of the sour note, but we're all good friends so let me try. After I had been at Cal two years I was visited by two very esteemed members of the faculty who said to me, "Jim, you've been recommended to us as a candidate for promotion to full professor and one of the criteria we must look at in connection with this is your teaching ability. We know what you've written and what research you're doing, etc. Now we'd like to come and visit your class on Wednesday at 4 o'clock to evaluate your teaching." And I said, "Gee, that will be great. I'd just love to have you. Let me tell you what this seminar is. I have about 15 graduate students and for this particular Wednesday three or four of them have been working on a particular project; they've done some research on it and they're going to be reporting their findings; there are three other students who have been working on another problem and they also will be reporting. I'll conclude by leading a discussion on implications of the results of the two investigations. The head of the two-member team said, "Well, let us know when you're teaching."

I think this illustrates that by and large at the college level we traditionally think that *teaching is lecturing*. The same still is true at the secondary-school level. I've had a chance for the last two years to move around the country and look at experimental teacher education programs and at the impact these new programs are having on the kind of teaching new trainees do. I came away with a very distinct impression, after visiting hundreds of high schools, that in all too many cases *teaching is talking*. Then, more recently, I've had the opportunity to be in the South to observe Negro colleges, Negro high schools, and Negro elementary schools. I've come away with the impression that the model that we have there is that *teaching is preaching*. Now I'm wondering, as a result of what we have seen today, whether or not we're centering our attention on a new model: *teaching is presenting*. This is my question.

BUSH: That's a good question and I think a valid criticism of the part that refers to the active behavior of the teacher only. This is part of the reason I referred to the need for a holistic approach that goes along concurrently, in which you have developmental case studies, in which you look at the total teacher as he's developing over a period of time to prevent precisely what you are speaking of. On the other hand, if the teacher is going to persist in talking, he ought to be trained to talk properly, to ask the right questions, and not to carry on in blind imitation of the models he's had for so long from us in the colleges—which is now the case. I don't subscribe to the proposition that the best way to conduct education is to put young people in a room and wait to see what happens. Teaching, which is what we are studying, is a process whereby a skilled person tries to help a less skilled person develop competence. We are interested in *the activity of the teacher*. It may be that one of the behaviors we want to study is for the teacher to be quiet. That may be a very good behavior at times. O.K.?

SCHUELER: In line with that, I wonder whether it would be possible to turn the whole thing around a little bit. Inevitably, teachers tend to teach somewhat as they were taught. Is there any possibility of using these techniques that you're developing for the improvement of teaching in teacher education?

BUSH: We have been. What I presented today represents a team approach. For example, the reason that Fred [McDonald] and Dwight [Allen] and Norm [Boyan] and others can talk interchangeably on this problem is that as we all teach our trainees; when one of us is teaching, the others are observing. We make audio and visual recordings of our teaching. After one gets over the chilling effect, it is good to have your colleagues' interest and criticism. It has been most stimulating to me in attempts to improve my own teaching. It has contributed to my enjoyment of teaching.

BOYAN: Mr. Schueler might be interested in knowing that every once in awhile we even have the interns fill out the Stanford Teacher Appraisal Guide on our own teaching.

ALLEN: We have also been invited by a number of university departments here on the Stanford campus to come and make video recordings of the teaching of other professors in the academic departments and to participate with them in critiquing their performance.

AUDIENCE (Unidentified): Is there anything going on at the elementary level in this experimentation?

SCHUELER: Yes, we're doing this at Hunter.

BROUDY: Mr. Davies, I didn't want to end this discussion on a sour note. I have some appreciative remarks to make about Mr. Bush's presentation but I'll cut them to just one point, if I may. I think aside from the use of the technology for pedagogical self-examination, which I think is excellent, the technology enables us to do something that programmatically is really very impressive. As I watched the demonstration, it became clear to me that at Stanford you are making a distinction, which I think has been long overdue, among laboratory instruction, clinical instruction, and internship. These have all been lumped together into student-teaching, usually taking place in a classroom. Historically this has been due to poverty and many other circumstances, but this has been one of our great weaknesses, because we had to carry on all three kinds of instruction in a situation which was really adapted to only one, viz., internship.

The laboratory experience is a highly schematized version of the whole task and, as we saw, with electronic equipment it is possible to abstract from a total skill performance and practice that. The clinical experience is a molar experience; it uses a real case but need not involve a whole classroom. In a clinic one sees a typical case being handled by a master, so to speak. Laboratory and clinical activities can be carried on at the university, under the control of the teacher-training faculty. Because a classroom must be used for the internship, it may have to be conducted off-site. This is the most expensive part of the training on the specialized level in terms of space, personnel, and time. The release of actual classrooms from use for the observational and clinical phases is important.

There's only one question at this time that I would ask you about your work. As I watched the tapes, I was asking myself: "How much does the student have to know about the research that you people at Stanford are doing as his skills are being changed? Is he the pigeon in the Skinner box and is the knowledge of the theory in you, or is it within him, too?" This is the question I would want answered before characterizing this as professional training rather than simply skill conditioning.

BUSH: May I respond to the thoughtful way in which you put your finger on a very important point by saying this: If I had

had the time I would have delineated how we're trying to develop in the teacher the capacity to be a solver of the problems of teaching. We feel that it's necessary for him really to possess the knowledge and the theory so that he will join us as partners in this team for conducting on-going research. This is one of the most important features of what we are attempting: so to train beginning teachers that they will continuously research their own teaching. We want to shape behavior, yes; but most important we want to make critical problem-solvers of the people we're preparing. That is the essence, I think, of the presentation.

ADJOURNMENT

Chapter III

Making Teacher Education Meaningful in Urban Settings

By Herbert Schueler
President
Richmond College
City University of New York*

A teacher education program is, and must be, judged by the performance of its products. This makes the practitioner in teacher education infinitely more vulnerable than some of his colleagues in the so-called liberal arts who find noble refuge behind the delusion that their efforts prepare for life and not a living. The teacher-educator has no such escape, and even if he sought it, his critics, among them his Olympian colleagues in the liberal arts, but above all the testimony in word and deed of the teachers he has helped fashion, would never allow him to find it. No part of a teacher's professional preparation can be justified as an end in itself; it must in some meaningful way contribute to his functioning as a teacher in a real community, in a specific school, with pupils who have tangible, not ideal, existence, who are what they happen to be, not what dwellers in ivory towers contend they should be. The study of the child is of little moment in a professional curriculum unless it contributes to the understanding of children who can be seen, felt, and worked with; no study of method is of use unless it helps fashion properly an effective teaching style for the teacher; no study of the social foundations of education can be justified

---

*Mr. Schueler was Director of Teacher Education, Hunter College, City University of New York, at the time this paper was presented. His address was accompanied with the presentation of slides and audio tapes illustrating the problems and frustrations of the typical teacher-trainee in a big-city setting.

unless it can be put to service in understanding the interactive dynamics of the schools and the communities in which its students are going to serve as teachers. This is not to say that we should forsake generalization for the particular, that in being preoccupied with the pebble we should neglect the beach, that in emphasizing the practical we should forsake ennobling theory. Far from it; yet as developers of practitioners we must be judged by what our products do, and our contribution to their proper functioning and being as professionals is the only justification of our existence. The verities of teacher education may on occasion seem eternal, but they should never be out of this world.

Let us consider, therefore, the world of the teacher in an urban society, and for the sake of analysis at the very least, consider the problem *de novo,* as if no academic university traditions existed, as if we were faced with the opportunity of fashioning a new teacher education program based on the needs of a specific school system in a specific urban society, with pupils as we now find them, and with potential teachers as we now discover are eligible and available. This analysis will be based of course on a city and population I know best, but I leave it to you to judge whether it will provide analogies for other cities and the needs of other urban populations. I suspect there are many such analogies, for our land, particularly in its developing urban aspects, is showing many more similarities than differences, and while specifics may vary, they fall into significantly similar patterns. It is becoming increasingly difficult to tell one city in our land from another, particularly in the problems it spawns. Urbanization and the burgeoning of population caught in the despond of poverty and deprivation seem, alas, to be two sides of the same leaden coin, and their depressed currency has made reluctant bedfellows of us all.

Let us consider therefore the largest of our cities and its children; the public schools that are expected to provide them with the stimulation and counsel that will, in our best democratic tradition, provide them with the help they need to ascend to the place in productive society that their will and talent make possible; and the young college students in training to become the teachers who will guide them. Who are these children, and who are these future teachers?

It is estimated that by 1970 the more than a million children enrolled in the public schools of this largest of our cities will by an overwhelming majority, seven out of ten, to be exact, be of a socioeconomic background that must be classified as disadvantaged—children of poverty, of deprivation, living for the most part in that most degrading of urban environments, the teeming, cheerless slum, the grey, polluted ghetto, the breeder of crime, delinquency, and numbing despair. One may bemoan the forces that have brought this accelerating condition about— the immigration of the displaced poor from rural areas no longer able or willing to sustain them; the evil of bigotry driving the displaced to a promised land unable to fulfill its promise; the accelerated birthrate that always seems to afflict the children of poverty, causing more to compete for the same scraps of sustenance that starved their fathers; the profiteering sins of the slum lord, the loan shark, the dope pusher, the gang leader; the declining market for the unskilled; and the industrial automation that is making unneeded great armies of the semiskilled. But the fact remains that the disadvantaged are there, that they are fast becoming majority populations in our decaying inner cities, and that they desperately need help. Though they represent the majority population in most of our public schools, they belong to those we consider to be minorities—the Negro and the Puerto Rican.

That crime and delinquency fester in their midst is undeniable. It is inevitable that some of the deprived will attempt to feed on the more fortunate; that the passions of the disadvantaged will be whipped to lawlessness by the exploiters of the poor; that the deceptively easy way of crime will appeal to some who bear the stigma of futile battle with the way of virtue that often is far from its own reward in the culture of poverty. It is undoubtedly true that as many as 75 percent of the individuals in the worst slum areas may be dependent on public assistance for the necessities of living, and that a significant number are members of families that for generations have subsisted on relief. It is true also that there are distressingly many children of broken homes, children who were born out of wedlock, children who have known none of the benign security of paternal and maternal love; children who have never known what it means to be a child, who have had the awesome responsibilities and terrors of adulthood thrust upon them years before their normal time. All this and more is abundantly true; and lest we forget it, the press, dedicated to what it considers newsworthy—and what sells papers better than reports of crime? —will keep reminding us that it is true. It is happening, and it is getting worse rather than better. To this unsavory chronicle are added reports of incidents of defiance directed against teachers, even occasional reports of bodily harm.

But there is also another side, a side of positive normalcy, which, being normal, rarely reaches notice, even if in sum it most certainly outweighs the negative that feeds the headlines and the prejudice of those blessed with greater fortune. As if economic, social, and cultural disadvantage were not enough of a handicap, the reputation of the urban slum dweller, however virtuous, God-fearing, and diligent he may be, is blackened before the world by the unsavory crimes of a minority of his kind. His children are condemned out of hand as potential delinquents because sensation-mongering newspaper compilations make school vandalism and defiance seem commonplace. It is a fact known by few but criminologists and some sociologists that many an offense perpetrated by a youngster of "good" family in the middle-class suburbs rarely becomes a case on the police blotter, while a similar offense by a delinquent in the slums almost inevitably does. Though the deeds may be similar, the difference in treatment by the police, and therefore the difference in delinquency statistics, may be considerable. There are stable families in slums as well as in suburbs, obedient children, loving and devoted parents, exemplars of morality, church-goers, job-holders, and law-respecting citizens. There are also families and individuals who would aspire to the economic stability that steady employment affords who are prevented by circumstances, lack of education, or just downright prejudice from attaining what they desperately desire. Indeed, we have just begun to recognize that for every family that has succumbed for several generations to the bare subsistence security of relief, there is another that, though clearly eligible, puts

82

pride before acceptance of what it considers degrading charity, and struggles along on its own.

Romantic notions to the contrary notwithstanding, there is no virtue in poverty, particularly the kind that festers in our cities; it is all the more remarkable that so much virtue is maintained in spite of this poverty and its consequent degrading conditions of living. It is to be expected that evil lurks in our slums; what is heartening is that so much virtue survives in spite of it.

That the majority of the children and youth enrolled in public schools in our city live in disadvantaged economic and social circumstances can be documented, and at least the realization, if not the cure, is clear. Less clear, less prone to statistical representation, are the ethnic and cultural characteristics and the life styles of the many kinds of children of the inner city. Most obviously different, but not necessarily by this token properly understood, are the life styles of the Puerto Rican urban migrants. Distinctive in language and dress, different in patterns of family living, tradition, and custom, they have transformed large areas of the city into Latin enclaves as foreign to the older established mainland culture as anything that the traveler can visit in this hemisphere. Indeed, to the middle-class mainlander, there may be much more that is familiar and understandable to him in the city of San Juan than in Spanish Harlem, even though the latter can be reached by a short subway ride from his home. More complex are the life styles of the Puerto Rican's immediate urban neighbor, the Negro, whose burgeoning population is an uneasy, sometimes explosive admixture of second- and third-generation Northerners with newer immigrants from the South, who though similar in color may be as foreign in custom to their Northern brothers as are their Puerto Rican neighbors down the street. Add to these the many other ethnic groups—Eastern European, Oriental, Middle Eastern—that have found uneasy haven in the teeming tenements catering to those of the poorest means, and you have the majority population served by the urban public schools.

If this is the population of the schools, who are their teachers; and of greater moment for the future, who are the students aspiring to become their teachers? One fact is obvious:

They do not live in the neighborhoods whence come their students. Their station in life, however modest in comparison with other professions requiring training of comparable duration and qualifications of comparable level, is still a considerable cut above the state of economic and social disadvantage that entraps their students. The neighborhood they are supposed to serve is therefore not their home; at most it is a path to be trod on their way to and from work. Therefore the social acquaintance of the teacher in the suburbs or small town with the neighbors whose children he teaches—in home, market, theater, church, beauty parlor, bridge club, bowling alley—is not a normal part of the urban teacher's everyday life. The life of the urban teacher's students is not within his economic sphere, nor is it within his social and cultural circumstance and aspiration. In almost every meaningful particular, he is not of their kind. Even those few among them who were able to use the profession of teaching to rise above the disadvantage of their birth and upbringing, and who now return to teach the children of a society from which they have escaped, experience this problem of fundamental difference, but in a particularly complex way. For the circumstance of their once having been a part of the society whose children they now are expected to guide does not necessarily give them the ability or the will to meet the children at the children's level; in fact, it may indeed handicap them much more than their colleagues from across the river, who do not have the psychological problem of having to relive the state from which they have escaped.

For the foreseeable future, however, the teachers of the urban public school child will continue to emerge not from the ghettoes of the decaying city, not from the ranks of the disadvantaged, not from the minorities that form the emerging majorities of registrants in the urban school, but from the more privileged, better housed, lower-middle and middle classes. And they will continue to be different from their pupils in background, custom, and life-style. A look at the populations of our teacher-preparatory universities makes this abundantly clear. Even those large public urban universities established to provide higher education for the deserving regardless of economic circumstance find themselves, in spite of minimal or no tuition, with student populations representative not of the disadvantaged who need them most, and for whom the path to the professions is thereby forever closed, but of the middle class.

This lack of representation of children of the disadvantaged in the student population of the colleges and universities is probably the most dramatic example of the accelerating process of social class immobility that is becoming characteristic of urban lower socioeconomic classes. In fact, the process of education that represents the traditional American hope of attaining that quality of opportunity we hold most dear seems to be failing the population that needs it most. There is clear evidence that the longer the child of the ghetto remains in school the further below the norm he will find himself in the attainment of fundamental scholastic skills. It seems almost as if schooling retards rather than quickens his development. Yet in spite of this, the school remains his major hope. Without it and the training it provides he can never liberate himself from the disadvantaged state that produced him and combat the deprivations that beset him. True, better housing, social services, job opportunities, all are needed; but none of these can supplant the school and the guidance and training it can provide. The school is the one stable agency of social change that holds the key to restoring upward mobility to urban populations enmeshed in disadvantage and deprivation.

PROGRAM REQUIREMENTS

With this school population, therefore, and with these teachers, both present and potential; and with this critical mission of the school providing the object, subject, and goal of teacher education, what manner of program needs to be developed? One thing is clear: It cannot be developed in an ivory tower apart and remote from the people it is intended to serve, and from the conditions in which they live. It has never been so demonstrably true that the process of education can begin only from the place where people are, rather than from the ideal state where it is fondly and vainly hoped they should be, or where our faulty memories suppose we once were. This means that the fashioners of curricula for teacher education must go back to school, not to the school that they and most of their

85

students in their comfortable middle-class provincialism know so well, but to the school of the inner city and the neighborhood and people it serves.

To many it will be more foreign than the communities they know abroad as summer tourists; to most it will reveal the significant extent to which the university community has largely ignored even the outwardly observable facts of urban change. It is time they experienced and studied the faces and life-styles of the communities that need the teachers they are going to train. And it is time they visited the schools in these communities observing at firsthand the youngsters and their teachers and the requirements of teaching that have as their base the ethnic and social class characteristics of the children of the inner city.

In addition, they should make a particular point of discovering what the teachers themselves conceive of as their mission, their problems, their successes, and their frustrations, both as they reveal the appropriateness of the prior training they have received and their needs for further training and assistance. To those who have tried this exercise, it has never failed to be revealing and disturbing in the magnitude and complexity of the unfulfilled tasks it has uncovered and in the extent to which so much of the university's work in training teachers, and so much of school practice, is utterly inadequate to meet the needs of disadvantaged youth.

With these exercises in humility as a frame of reference, the curriculum of teacher education must be examined anew, both in its preparatory and its in-service aspects. It is already apparent that the discipline of pedagogy will need the assistance not only of its old friend psychology but also that of sociology, social psychology, and cultural anthropology. It is apparent, too, that many of the examples and illustrations and even principles of proper school practice held most dear by textbooks and professors of teaching method are as foreign to the requirements of teaching in the inner city as the middle-class, surburban Spot, Dick, Jane of our basal readers are alien to the child of the teeming tenement.

The test of appropriateness in a program of training content is its relevance to the use it is expected to fulfill. Therefore the social foundations content of teacher education geared to urban service must provide a basis for understanding the forces of urban society; the characteristics of its many kinds of people and the dynamics of their life-style. Similarly, the pedagogical content of teacher education must be relevant to the personal and social characteristics of the learners it is expected to serve and must take into account the differences in social and ethnic class and custom between teacher and pupil. The customs, value systems, and modes of behavior of his students must be known to the teacher before he can operate with them, particularly if they are different from his own. In dealing with and guiding the behavior of his pupils, the teacher must know and understand their personal, social, and human motivations and determinants. In short, he must understand his student and the living, real environment, physical and human, of which he is a part.

This is no easy task for the curriculum builder of teacher education. He will need all the help he can get from the social worker, the cultural anthropologist, the social psychologist, the sociologist. He will need to take his examples, his case studies, his problems, more and more from the world in which his students will be teaching. He will use these schools as his laboratory, as the subject and object of his teaching.

In any professional training program, direct observation and practice go hand in hand with vicarious study. It is expected that these direct experiences will not only provide the practical application for foundational study but gradually will build understanding and skill in operating within the ultimate conditions of this service. One's practice in training, to be effective, must be relevant to what he will meet as a professional. If teaching in an urban public school is his professional goal, then a significant proportion of his laboratory observation and practice should be in such a school. While it may be more convenient, gracious, satisfying, and less fraught with unfamiliar frightening problems to use as the laboratory of teacher education the so-called "good" middle-class school familiar to both professor and future teacher, it is the height of absurdity to expect the teacher to learn his craft in surroundings so alien to those he will be expected to serve. If the future teacher is being prepared to serve in the schools of the city, a significant proportion of his training should be in these schools. His learning about the children of the slums will remain academic unless he has the opportunity to be in their company; he cannot learn to be their teacher if his observation and practice are with others quite different.

Programs of teacher education with similar goals need not follow the same patterns as long as they accomplish common objectives. Thus undergraduate programs that culminate in student teaching and programs that postpone professional training to the first post-baccalaureate years may be equally as effective in training for urban service, as long as the materials of study and the practical induction into teaching are focused squarely on the realistic requirements of the urban school. So demanding are these requirements, however, that a much more gradual induction into teaching is indicated, together with an intensified, functional continuing program of further in-service training. The all-too-common practice of thrusting full-time, largely unsupervised teaching responsibility on the neophyte fresh from the relatively sheltered environment of student-teaching or the first-time exposure to practice in a part-time internship is far too fragmentary an induction into urban teaching service. A gradual progression from observation to participation as an aide, to student-teaching, to internship, to closely supervised part-time teaching, to teaching as the junior member of a closely knit team of professionals, to self-reliant service as a regular teacher, should take several years of carefully planned and supervised development, using the resources of both school and university in functioning partnership. At present, far too many new teachers are thrust prematurely into full teaching responsibility with a minimum of concurrent help. The result is inevitable: for many disillusionment, for some abandonment of the profession, for others descent into a demeaning level of service not too different from bare custodial care and a classroom run more on the lines of a prison than a school.

Conditions change, neighborhoods change, people change, knowledge changes, and the needs of people and society change. Teachers, like other professionals in medicine, law, engineering, social work, and business, should be expected to be continuously responsive to these changes. Yet too often the achievement of full certification (attainable in the most advanced of our systems during the very first years of service) is the practical end of training other than that provided by the amassing of experience. This stultifying attitude is behind many of the failures of teachers adequately trained for earlier conditions to cope with rapidly changing environments and pupils, often in the very same school. Particularly for the urban public school teacher, knowledge of the developing neighborhood and the environment of his pupils is indispensable to his effectiveness. As the environment changes he must be helped to gain anew a needed knowledge and understanding of his clientele. In fact, no teacher newly appointed to an urban neighborhood, however stable and successful his prior experience, can function properly without such specific new knowledge. Changing clientele, changing neighborhoods, changing needs, require changes in school practice, in curriculum, in materials. The time is long past when the textbook slave could survive in the urban public school. The teacher, not the publisher, needs to become more and more the agent of curriculum development in response to the distinctive needs and backgrounds of his pupils. Curriculum, therefore, as well as the related study of neighborhood and its people, is another imperative for continuing study by the urban teacher. This suggests the organization of professional service in such a way that some portion, built in during the regular schedule of paid service, be reserved for further study and consultation. This need for continuing study is too crucial to be left, as it now is, entirely to overtime attendance in courses after regular working hours and during summer recesses. Some of it, particularly that crucial portion relating directly to the teacher's effectiveness in the classroom, needs to become part of his job.

The needs of the city and its people must be central to any program for urban teacher education. The training of the teacher must be relevant to the services he is expected to provide and responsive to the pupils he is to teach. As the city changes, as its people change, as the state of knowledge and the world changes, so must the schools change and the requirements of teaching change. Perhaps the great failure of the urban public school and the universities that trained its teachers is their reluctance to change with the times. The problems of our cities and their schools cannot be met by looking wistfully backward, or elsewhere, or acting as if by ignoring them they might go away. Nor can the needs of the disadvantaged in our cities be met by condescension, resentment, disdain, and universally applied penal measures. Nor can the schools and their teachers ignore their proper function to provide the only really effective means of upward mobility for the children of poverty and deprivation. This requires a corps of dedicated, realistically trained teachers who find fulfillment and satisfaction in working where they are most needed. While their number is increasing, and while schools and universities are beginning to develop programs for their proper training, the commitment continues to fall short of accelerating need. There is hope, however, that the tide will turn, spurred on by the idealism of American youth, so dramatically demonstrated in the Peace Corps, for example, and the awakening awareness of schools and universities.

Discussion of the Schueler Paper

BOYAN: I was thinking, as I heard the tape and looked at the pictures Mr. Schueler showed us, that for every one of the sample situations paraded before us I personally have seen a parallel in middle-class schools, upper middle-class schools, and just about every type of school there is. So my first reaction is that what Mr. Schueler has let us in on is something which is not unique to the urban slum school. However, those of you who have had some experience in slum schools will recognize that these were merely illustrations and what is unique is their regularity, their consistency and constancy, and their amount. The teacher is unable to escape from that situation. It is in the quantitative aspect, I think, more than the qualitative aspect, of these kinds of situations that we see the distinct and unique characeristic of the urban slum school which teachers find extremely difficult to cope with. The burden of Mr. Schueler's remarks, his argument, is that if we can help teachers to understand the territory in which they work, they therefore will do a better job.

This is really the burden of all teacher education programs, as indeed it should be. The description which he has given us of a prototype of teacher preparation program for the urban slum schools holds as powerfully for the preparation of teachers for all schools. We should understand children better; we should understand the circumstances in which they live and operate. We should understand the backgrounds from which they come, the things that motivate them, their aspirations, the problems of life that they have to contend with going to and from school, and the like. The notion of preparing a teacher well for dealing with the reality shock of living in the situation holds as vigorously for the preparation of youngsters' teachers in Palo Alto as it does for Ravenswood; it holds as powerfully and as vigorously for Scarsdale as it does for Harlem.

Now there is one basic assumption that I would quarrel with; namely, that realistic training itself will lead to the fulfillment and satisfaction of the teacher who works in the urban slum schools. My hunch is that no amount of realistic training, no matter how good it is and how appropriate it is, will help a person sustain the consistent punishment which he receives in the urban slum school. This is reversing the argument from the usual position which says that teachers punish students. This is taking the position that pupils' behavior punishes teachers and that you can take just so much punishment. The military has recognized this and it rotates the troops. Even the Peace Corps, which as Mr. Schueler suggests has the idealism which we wish to capture in dedicated teachers, rotates its people. So perhaps we have to take the position that this is a war and that there is a shock for the teacher who has aspirations which go beyond that particular situation; that if he doesn't have aspirations to go beyond that particular situation, perhaps he shouldn't be a teacher at all.

So, perhaps we need to devise a scheme of using people which is different from what we now have, on top of the notion of developing realistic training. All of us want to develop realistic training programs whether we're pointing toward the middle-class school, the upper-class school, the Andovers, the Exeters, or the George Washington High Schol in Harlem or the William Penn and Ben Franklin schools I saw in Philadelphia. All of us want to devise programs of realistic training, and in each of these we do want to help people deal with the reality shock of the situation in which they work. But, what kind of injection of knowledge, what kind of injection of understanding, what kind of injection of dedication can we find to use as a treatment to help people learn to get satisfaction out of continuously punishing experiences? Perhaps the injection is one which would let them treat these experiences as not being punishment. I doubt that this can be done.

DAVIES: Mr. Schueler mentioned the National Teacher Corps proposal. This program is an opportunity to devise new kinds of training programs for young people to teach in the slum schools. Colleges and universities will offer three-month training programs, after which the interns will work in the schools with supervision. What would you envision, if you had your way, Mr. Schueler, to be the major substantive elements of the three-month preparation programs.

SCHUELER: Well, it's more than a three-month preparation program. That's another one of those mistakes. I was on an advisory board for the preparation of the bill and at first there was to be a quick, hopefully painless, injection of three months of something and then the teacher would go right in there and teach his heart out. The bill does, however, provide not only for a three months' initial experience but also for a year's part-time internship experience in which one-half of the time of the teacher will be devoted to training in the school in which he is teaching, or the neighborhood in which he is teaching, with the cooperation of the university, and then a follow-up of another year of gradually assuming full-time service with continuing supervision and help in whatever scheme—and this is left open—each locality may decide to experiment with. So it's not the kind of thing in which you project fast and then go in and bring the law to the heathen. It's an attempt to try to get young people with some commitment to work with teachers who have found some success and satisfaction in working in urban schools. You get them together and, with the help of trained university personnel, bring them to this position—not the way the Peace Corps does, give two years of your life and then leave—but as a longer, hopefully lifetime, commitment. There was an earlier version of the bill, the Edward Kennedy version, which attempted to use the Peace Corps rationale; that is, "Teachers of the nation, arise, give a year of your life for the disadvantaged and then leave."

If there is anything I will oppose as far as I can it's a rotation of teachers in and out of depressed areas as a sort of a punishment, or sometimes accompanied by an extra few hundred dollars in compensation. I will have to say in opposition to what you have said that there are teachers in practically every urban slum school that I know, and I know an awful lot of them, who are highly effective and seem not only to survive but also find professional stimulation enough to remain there. There are others who consider it a punishment. The problem is not, believe me, just of quantity of punishment. There are other problems there. I tried to make the point that this constant harping on how difficult life is, what the kids will do to you, what's going to happen to you, and how you should never be found in the neighborhood after dark, by constant harping on these disadvantages of teaching in the urban schools we are doing more harm than good. There's an awful lot that is positive even in slum schools.

Classroom problems of slum schools are of concern to us because they have largely been teacher-inspired and not pupil-inspired. They have arisen because the teacher was not skilled in recognizing the motivations behind the behavior and was not skilled enough to handle the behavior problems. There is one big factor which differentiates slum school problems from those of suburban middle-class schools. That is the type of person the teacher is. He is not the kind of person his pupils are. There is not only a vertical difference, the difference between age and experience; there is the horizontal difference of social class, ethnic background, and aspirations; and this makes the training problem and the teaching problem such a crucially distinctive one. We have all along acted as if we can prepare teachers for everywhere if we only have a good program. If we take that attitude we prepare them for *nowhere*; you *have* to be specific.

BROUDY: It occurs to me that two things are very distressing about the whole thing. One is the apparent magnitude of the problem and the other is the role of the teacher. Gunnar Myrdal's theory of cumulative change may be a source of, if not optimism, then alleviation of the pessimism. Myrdal said that when we have a problem which has many variables, as this problem has, and if these variables are related to each other, if we push hard in every direction possible and are patient, the take-off point will be reached, and we will get a chain reaction that produces dramatic results. For example, if the poverty legislation really begins taking hold and the economic condition of these people begins to improve this would interact reciprocally with all the other variables. We might get a very dramatic success. In other words, Myrdal seems to advise us never to get trapped into saying: "Don't pass a law because this in itself won't do it," or "Don't improve education because this in itself won't do it."

As to preparing teachers adequate to the situation, I am speaking from hunches and not from any solid base of evidence, but I have asked myself, "How has society found personnel to cope with a great many social tasks which are unpleasant and even painful?" I have in mind finding morticians to deal with the dead, or slaughterhouse personnel to handle intestines and blood. I'm thinking of the practical nurse who may have to empty bedpans and clean up a patient three times within an hour. How do these people do it? Sometimes it's through dedication, although the dedication to be a slaughterhouse worker, I would guess, is not very common. There seems to be something else. Perhaps it's *routinization*. Nothing is intolerable if one has a method for doing it, and after a while routine depersonalizes the act. I suspect that part of the training of personnel in this and other areas where the circumstances are unpleasant ought to be the development of routines that keep personnel from being involved so intimately and personally as the teacher seems to be in the tape that we heard.

Another factor is intellectualization. Again, if you'll forgive a crude example, a pathologist examines feces; so does a practical nurse, and so does someone who has to clean latrines. I suggest it's the intellectualization of the task and the means of accomplishing it that matters. Routinization plus intellectualization equals professionalization.

MORK: I'd like to ask Mr. Schueler a question following this line. I have heard many talks, as I'm sure many of you have, referring to but not describing the qualities needed by teachers who work with the deprived—personality qualities and skills if they are to work effectively. Can you tell us what some of them are? I think we need to know. We have a small program of this sort going in our university and I find it terribly difficult to get any response to this question. I realize what a difficult question it is, but every time I have the opportunity I like to probe.*

BOYAN: Could I make the stipulation, as Mr. Schueler describes these qualities, that he indicate whether they are unique to slum school situations or general to all teachers?

SCHUELER: Well, here again I can't go along with that way of argument. There may be general principles and general qualities like being empathic with youngsters that are required of all teachers. But the requirement will change as soon as it becomes specific, as soon as you have to talk about a given teacher and a given group of youngsters. If one says that a teacher must have a charismatic quality, it applies to all situations. But to achieve it with this given group of youngsters may be an entirely different problem than to achieve it with another. The situation itself brings in variables. For example, some of the things which you heard on the tape were selections chosen for negative effect. We also have some very positive ones. The tapes you heard seem to reveal a lack not only of understanding of the motivation for the children's behavior but also a lack of caring about these motivations. The thinking is first of the teacher's well-being and only secondly of the children's well-being. Now here again one can argue that obviously all teachers have to be selfless. But some teachers can achieve it in one situation but cannot achieve it in another. One reason for taking as a baseline the absolute necessity of knowing as much as you can find out and understand about the neighborhoods in which the youngsters live—their family backgrounds, and the problems of the youngsters themselves—is that this is but a first step and you can't go anywhere until you take that first step; because if you cannot fashion your action on the basis of knowledge of what kind of a background the child has, then the chances are pretty good that you're going to fail right then and there.

What makes the slum situation distinctive from the non-slum situation is, first, that the young people we are getting

---

* Since this discussion was conducted, William W. Wayson has published a summary of his dissertation ("Expressed Motives of Teachers in Slum Schools," University of Chicago, 1966) in the May, 1966, *Administrator's Notebook* under the title, "Sources of Teacher Satisfaction in Slum Schools."—*The Editor*.

for teacher training know practically nothing from their natural background about these conditions and about these children. Secondly, I would say that there are certain elements that are more crucial in working with this kind of population than there are with other populations. You can get away with much more in a non-slum situation with non-deprived children without necessarily damaging the child than you can in the slum, because in no place is the school so desperately needed as in the slum. In the suburban populations you've got greater support from other agencies in the community, including the education of the parents and their levels of aspiration and the push one gets from the community. In the slum the school is the only agency that has the potential of doing something about this. Therefore, a failure in the slum school is a much greater failure. It is a much greater social failure, not only to society but to the child, than is a similar failure in a suburban school. And here is where you get your difference.

I would say further that I would never require any teacher to teach in an area or in a school that he doesn't want to teach in. You cannot force people to like to teach if you say, "All right, you prefer to be there but you stay here." We're very much worried about that in some of our programs in the City of New York and various of our teacher-education programs for slum schools. But we discovered a very interesting thing: When we made it voluntary, when we offered alternatives, when we indicated that here we were going to try to help the individual as much as possible in what is a very difficult situation, we got the volunteers. It's the commitment that they themselves bring that helps. Without that you can't do the job. Imagine what kind of teachers you got out of this rotating business—you know, in New York City, for awhile, if you ever wanted to become a candidate for a supervisory license you had to "do time" for two years in the slum schools.

COGAN: May I make two points? One is to emphasize the utility of understanding, of knowledge, in the training of teachers. I really think that we need to say something about the relationship between knowledge and behavior and the relationship between visceral response and behavior, and I'm sure I don't have to elaborate that point. The second point is in direct accord with your argument against rotation. It is that it may be possible to add to the list of people who *do* tolerate jobs like this, i.e., pathologists, nurses, people who work in slaughter-houses; it may be possible to add to that list people like sociologists, doctors who work in clinics, policemen who work in these deprived areas. If we ask ourselves what the doctors and sociologists find to keep them there, the truth is that they have not merely intellectualized; they have translated the problems that they face into *professional* problems. The handle them with self-knowledge. It's the lack of self-knowledge that causes so much of the teachers' discomfort. The professionalization and the self-knowledge a teacher needs—why he does what he does—may translate the whole thing into problem-solving in a sociologist's sense, or in a doctor's sense.

BELLACK: I think the schools still face the question, "What are we going to do in this total complex of institutions that influence the lives of children and youth?" I would be interested to hear you talk about the question of the curriculum. That is, what are you going to involve these youngsters in? As I listen to the tape it is obvious that the youngsters were not involved in anything that we would consider educational. I was reminded of a study that Professor Phil Jackson has completed at the University of Chicago in which he interviewed teachers who were judged to be very successful. He asked them, "What are your greatest satisfactions in teaching? What is the thing that makes you feel good about what you are doing?" As he analyzed the interviews it became very obvious that the thing that gave them the greatest satisfaction was to help students become involved in significant intellectual activities and worthwhile enterprises. So I think part of the question is, "What are you going to get these youngsters involved in and toward what end?" We have been talking this evening about specialization. What is the curriculum problem this poses?

SCHUELER: We cannot separate the training of teachers from the curriculum in which they're going to be involved, and that is one reason for the statement that a much larger proportion of the teacher's preparation for pre-service and in-service should be directed toward the assumption that he is going to be a primary agent in developing the curriculum with his youngsters. He can no longer say, "Now, what book can I use here, what book can I use there?" If he's going to reach youngsters who are in a certain environment, he has to build on what is around them and, if necessary, develop them above it. For example, the little moving excerpts at the end of the tape were part of a curriculum study program that is now in its fourth year, one of the Project English programs. We call it Gateway English. With the help of our own teacher-trainees and experts from the outside we're trying to develop curriculum materials in the language arts for the sixth, seventh, eighth, and the intermediate school grades that utilize aspirations and realistic environmental experiences of the youngsters themselves. There are lots of things that are very positive and there are lots of things that are needed very badly. For example, there is one very interesting little book which has the title *Coping*. Coping with problems as you meet them. There's another one that is called *Home*, and the message that the youngsters are supposed to gather from this in discussing it and reading other materials is that home is not necessarily just a place, because it isn't to them. Home to them is where they sleep, and this is not home in our sense. Therefore, home is not only places, it's people, a sense of belonging, etc. The whole set of learning materials and teaching materials has been developed around that theme, with children participating. And all along we hope that by having something that can be felt by children as vital to them we will enhance their scholastic skills. This should characterize the entire curriculum.

BUSH: I think it's quite clear that we're going to have to change the total condition in the city, which means we're going to have to change the total school condition. As suggested, many forces are going to be at work on this. It isn't simply a matter of training one set of teachers for urban schools and another set for rural schools. I think Mr. Schueler will agree with that. I would submit that what probably happens today is that our general failure in teacher education shows up most dramatically in the urban situation. If we had fully prepared teachers coming out of our programs, such as no doubt come out of Mr. Schueler's program, they would be able to teach in any kind of school. This is what we ought to have. This is not to gainsay that some might prefer to teach in one and some might prefer to teach in another kind of situation. But our sights ought to be raised to the level where a person could perform adequately, if he so wished, in different situations.

Mr. Broudy put his finger on one very important point: the lack in our teacher-training program. It shows up everywhere. One factor that makes teaching so demanding is the idea that a teacher must succeed with every pupil all of the time. It can't be done. A medical doctor who is working in an area where the incidence of a certain infectious disease is much higher than elsewhere doesn't consider that he's a failure if his rate is different than if he practiced somewhere else. We ought to realize this in our teacher-training programs.

AUDIENCE (Unidentified): Implementation of Title I [of the Elementary and Secondary Education Act of 1965] requires the availability of educational specialists. Do you see that the difference of opinion here could be resolved by the employment of resource teachers, specialists, educational aides, and educational clerks as relief valves for this thing that the teacher experiences in the classroom where there is a great burden on the teacher? Could these additional people serve as part of the relief valve we'd like to have?

BOYAN: I think there are two kinds of issues. The first is a restatement of what I tried to say that Mr. Bush brought out—good teacher-education programs are good teacher-education programs, and the pathology of the urban slum situation in many ways tends to highlight what we do well and what we don't do well and how people react to these things. That's one kind of thing. The second point that I feel really needs some further exploration, not only by Mr. Schueler and the people he is working with in New York City but by all the rest of us, is how you arrange the intellectual content of the training program and how you influence the behavior of teachers so that they will then get the kind of satisfaction out of working in difficult schools which will help sustain them. I think this probably is the key more than just understanding the domain in which the pupils live.

SCHUELER: Understanding the domain is just the first step.

ADJOURNMENT

Chapter IV

The Academic Major in the Education of Teachers

By Morris L. Cogan
Professor of Education and Chairman
Department of Teacher Education
University of Pittsburgh

Once upon a time long ago a conclave of rabbinical scholars became embroiled in an attempt to define the word "scholar." The discussion ended when an elder spoke up and said: "A scholar is like a pin, which must, as you know, have a good sharp end, as well as a good round end. The scholar's sharp end is to think with; his round end is to sit down to the job with."[1] The moral of this parable may perhaps be extended to fit the school-teacher, who needs the sharp end of scholarship to think with and the round end of professional education to sit down to his job with—and possibly to face his critics with.

Today almost everyone agrees on the necessity for scholarly breadth and depth in the education of teachers. Scholarship is "in." This near-consensus is one of the principal orthodoxies of contemporary thought in education. Like so many other orthodoxies, this one occasionally serves as a substitute for thought and action. A radical examination of the question may therefore be useful.

DEFINITIONS AND BOUNDARIES

The term "major" is taken here in the customary sense of a collegiate specialization: the candidate's principal study, in which he is required to complete a program of specified courses

---

[1] Adapted from a story told by A. Myerson in *Speaking of Man.* New York: A. A. Knopf, 1950, p. 7.

or credit hours. "Academic" major refers to the disciplines of the humanities, the natural sciences, and the social sciences as commonly offered in liberal arts colleges. These majors will be considered in relation to the education of both elementary and secondary school teachers. (The treatment of specializations for the teaching of home economics, vocational education, and similar non-academic studies offered in the public schools must be left to another occasion.) The terms used in this paper as synonyms of "major" will include "discipline," "specialization," and "subject speciality," with the adjectives, "academic" and "scholarly" often prefixed.

There is not much profit in attempting to specify the components of a major. Such programs are usually determined by each collegiate faculty and by the accidents of history. Recognizing this definitional problem, James B. Conant has suggested that we get rid of the "two mongrel academic terms 'major' and 'minor'." He suggests that we substitute "concentration" or "degree of concentration in a field or fields."[2] The latter perhaps implies a description in terms of courses taken, which would provide some specificity but would be cumbersome. But even so, none of the definitions of "major" convey the complex denotations and connotations of the concept. In truth, it is not mechanically definable in the barren sense that one can define, for example, "Carnegie unit." The quality of the instruction and still more the quality of the learning are the critical differentiae of a major in any event.

It should also be noted that although the academic professors generally hold the educationists responsible for the adulteration of the teacher's major, their own house is not in impeccable order. As Conant has written, a major does not always mean "depth," and the "conventional major is not, then, the dependable hallmark it is often thought to be," even in the prestigious colleges.[3] And B. O. Smith presses the point home when he notes that the explanation for weaknesses of the teacher's program "may lie in the fragmentation and disorder of the liberal

---

[2] *The Education of American Teachers.* New York: McGraw-Hill, 1962, p. 106.

[3] *Op. cit.,* p. 103.

arts curriculum . . ." where the courses seem with few exceptions to be "bred of the needs and interests of those who teach them" rather than of those who come to be taught.[4]

It is also worth noting that questions about the teacher's major must be addressed to the liberal arts colleges, since only a small fraction of our teachers come from teachers colleges.

WHY THE PRESENT CONCERN WITH SPECIALIZATION?

It is appropriate to inquire why there is such a strong resurgence of interest in the scholarly specialization of teachers. One reason is that a shift in the power structure of education has occurred. The education Establishment is in retreat before the academics in matters of the curriculum of the public schools and the program for the education of teachers. But it would be a mistake to view the movement for a return to academic excellence as merely a tightening of academic standards. And it would be equally a mistake to account for this state of affairs by supposing that the education Establishment has neglected academic scholarship in the preparation of teachers and that the academics, returned to power, are merely *restoring* scholarship to its rightful place. This is part of the story, but only a small part.

It is as much revulsion as revolution that has motivated the power takeover of the academics. It is revulsion against what Dennis Wrong has termed the "vocationalism, present-mindedness, and pallid middle-class conformism of a public education which is subject to all the bureaucratic and political pressures of our mass society."[5] The dislike of "Dick and Jane" literature is as much directed against conformism as against intellectual malnutrition. The retreat from mathematics as "a tool skill" is as much a reaction against vocationalism and anti-intellectualism as it is a thrust toward academic rigor. The key words in prescriptions for public education and its teachers have been "excellence" and "quality." The connotations of this use of "excellence" and "quality" include, it is true, scholarly rigor. But we

---

[4]"On the Preparation of Teachers" (undated mimeographed paper), pp. 3-4.

[5]Dennis H. Wrong, "Jews, Gentiles, and the New Establishment," *Commentary*, No. 6, Vol. 39, June, 1965, p. 84.

shall fail to understand the full implications of the contemporary revolution in education unless we comprehend that "excellence" connotes also the value given to intellectualism and the examined life of the mind. "Excellence" accounts for the emphasis on problem-solving and critical thinking, on the importance of creative and esthetic experience in learning. "Excellence" refers also to the affective and motivational components of schooling, e.g., discovery, intuition, and the important, "incidental," and usually unanticipated outcomes of instruction, e.g., gaining knowledge about oneself as a learner, and learning how to learn.

Such complex concerns underlie the objectives of the academicians for the education of teachers. What we shall have to watch for carefully in the future is whether the academicians hold themselves responsible for achieving such goals, or whether they rather relegate the task to the educators, or fall back on the stale cliché that teaching is an art and that teachers are born, not made. If they adopt the "born-not-made" posture, our only recourse will be to produce teachers by hatching them in eugenic marriages for the improvement of the breed.

Some Preliminary Perplexities

To subscribe to the idea of a "good, solid academic major" is not to solve the problem, it is only to uncover its complexities. The first complexity is the relation of the teacher's major to what he is actually called on to teach. If the objective of teaching is simply the induction of pupils into ever-deepening study of the academic disciplines, then it follows that the teacher can profit from more and more specialization in his major. But the objectives lie in part outside the domain of the disciplines. The schoolboy is expected to learn how to deal with both personal and societal problems that cut across and go beyond the academic specializations. And even *within* a field, like science for example, the teacher's task of relating chemistry to the other natural sciences demands a breadth of preparation that competes with the depth needed by the specialist. The emerging solution to this problem seems to be—and this is said without cynicism—to make the objectives of the school correspond ever more closely with the objectives of the collegiate disciplines. This trend is visible even in the elementary school. Here the increasing specialization made possible by programs of team teaching and the earlier introduction of "advanced" topics—intuitive algebra, for example—increase the teacher's dependence upon a rigorous college major.

The teacher's need for cross-disciplinary competences and for "non-disciplinary" wisdom, as required in the core curriculum or in general education, is popularly supposed to be met by the liberal studies, especially those of the first two undergraduate years. This seems to be a prime example of misplaced confidence. Most cross-disciplinary and general education teaching has been notably difficult to do well. It has had very little success at the collegiate and public school levels. This is attributed by some analysts to the lack of appropriate preparatory programs for the teachers. These analysts are quite possibly correct, but it is equally likely that the *personal* qualifications for such "generalist" teachers are rarely to be found. In brief, the specialist training of generalist teachers seems likely to remain the sphinx-like puzzle it now is.

Another and equally unsolved problem is the inadequate number of candidates for teaching who are academically strong enough to meet the demands of a rigorous college major. The likeliest solution seems to be to create a specially selected and trained corps of master teachers who will be capable of serving as leaders of teaching teams, as instructors for academically gifted students, as the moving force in the development and testing of the varied curricula, methods, and technology for the schools, and as the leaders for the internal evaluation and criticism so badly needed in the schools during this period of innovation. Both the *New York Times* and the *Saturday Review* seem convinced that such a new leadership corps is already in action at top national levels. Its counterpart is needed at the teacher's level throughout the nation's school systems.

The whole problem of the quality and quantity of teachers is well summarized by Robert E. Mason, who writes:

> There has been much careless talk about raising standards in teacher education. No responsible discussion of this

matter is possible except in direct relationship to specific and immediate considerations of teacher supply. Officials in the schools will, willy-nilly, hire good teachers if they can, poor teachers if they cannot.[6]

The implication of Mason's remarks is clear: It is irresponsible for anyone to speak of the necessary improvement in academic standards for teachers unless he is equally ready to set forth clearly and emphatically the inescapable responsibility of the society for the recruitment of adequate numbers of qualified men and women.

CHARACTERISTICS OF THE NEW MAJORS

It may be useful to examine some of the characteristics of the emerging programs for majors and to scrutinize the outcomes expected of them. What are to be the desired and desirable consequences of the new majors?

Competence in a Discipline

It is almost redundant to note that the first claim made for a good major is that it arms the teacher with adequate control of the subject matter he is to teach. The emphasis today, however, is not on the stale and unprofitable concept of mastery of all the important *facts* in a field of study. On the contrary, the question of competence in one's major becomes especially intriguing because the accelerating flood of knowledge makes mastery almost humanly impossible. It is therefore interesting to attempt to set down some of the principal dimensions of the emerging meanings of the phrase "competence in one's major field."

Perhaps the most frequent recommendation to be found in the literature on the programs for collegiate majors is the injunction to stress *selection, not "coverage."* This is easier said than done. Nevertheless, some academicians, notably in science,

---

[6] "Academic Standards and Professional Demands," *Teachers College Record*, Vol. 64, No. 5, February, 1963, p. 381.

are working productively to develop programmatic recommendations for teachers.[7]

A complementary dimension to the principle of selection rather than coverage is the idea that the teacher needs to have an understanding both of the "vast reaches" of his discipline and its limitations. He needs to know about the problems successfully met and solved, the failures, and the whole literature of speculation—the litany of what remains to be dreamed about.

If the teacher cannot truly "know" his major in the sense of the encyclopedic mastery of data, details, doctrines, principles, and laws, then it is clear that he must know, first the processes by which one *comes* to know in a discipline, and second, *which* knowledge promises him the greatest "mileage" in using what he knows and in learning what he does not yet know. To have command of the *processes by which one comes to know* means to command the tools and modes of analysis, the conceptual schemes by which one's discipline organizes itself, and the evidence and the logic on which conceptional frames are erected.

Both the teacher-scientist and the teacher-humanist need to know that the revolution in *scientific* knowing is paralleled by a revolution in *esthetic* or associative knowing. Thus we may know by way of a stream of consciousness, by observation of a slice of life, by cubistic or surrealistic art or "pop art" or "op art," by communication through jazz or through twelve-tone music or aleatory music. The reason why the teacher needs to know these modes of knowing are clear: Both he and his pupils may learn better or best through one or both modes.

As for the knowledge that gives the teacher the greatest economy and control of what he knows and in learning what he does not yet know, this has been popularized by Jerome Bruner as "structures." The word "structures" is an extremely useful metaphor, but like any good metaphor it may have many meanings. Some of the meanings that have been encountered include:

---

[7] A brief report on some of these endeavors may be found in *Foundations for Excellence*, the Fifteenth Yearbook of the American Association of Colleges for Teacher Education, 1962. Dorothy M. Fraser's "Current Curriculum Studies in Academic Subjects," published by the NEA in 1962, deals with the nationally important revisions of the public school curriculum.

the unifying ideas and concepts, those that are of most worth, that provide the greatest economy and elegance in organizing a discipline. For example, some of the "concepts and conceptual schemes which, along with other factors, organize biological knowledge and focus the direction of modern research are evolution, diversity of type and unity of pattern, generic continuity, complementarity of organism and environment . . . complementarity of structure and function . . ."[8] One interpretation of structures in the study of English is perhaps implied in the understanding of: "(a) the nature of language as an arbitrary signaling system; (b) the relation of language and culture; (c) the nature of correctness in speech and writing; and (d) . . . the sound structure, the morphological structure, and the syntactic structure of modern English."[9]

Alfred North Whitehead and Jerome Bruner were perhaps both speaking directly of structures and the education of teachers when Whitehead in 1917 inveighed against "inert knowledge" and "that passive reception of disconnected ideas," and Bruner in 1962 stated what has become the golden rule and the dominant theme of contemporary education, that "the structure of knowledge—its connectedness and the derivations that make one idea follow from another—is the proper emphasis in education."[10]

Only a few of the men and women working to develop programs of specialization speak of the teacher's need to know the *value systems*—scientific, esthetic, and moral—that form the context of a discipline and that have so strong an influence on its direction and development. A concern for such ideas reflects the need of the teacher to govern his conduct not solely by the internal scholarly ethic of his discipline, but to relate his conduct to a broader morality. Awareness of these concepts and of the need for governance by morality are evident in the moral

---

[8] E. Klinckmann, "New Curriculum Patterns for Biology Teachers," in *Foundations for Excellence, ibid.*, pp. 94-95.

[9] Cited from H. Allen, K. W. Dykema, and P. Roberts in G. R. Carlsen's "New Curriculum Patterns for English Teachers," in *Foundations for Excellence, ibid.*, p. 109.

[10] A. N. Whitehead, *The Aims of Education*. New York: Mentor Press, 1949; J. Bruner, "After John Dewey, What?" in *On Knowing: Essays for the Left Hand*, 1962, p. 120.

dilemmas of some atomic physicists as they view the consequences of their discoveries, and in the ethical problems created for many scholars by the conflict between their own views as to what research they really should be doing and the pressures of "directed" research money available from foundations and the government. In sum, the teacher needs to help his pupils comprehend that a discipline is rooted in its own ethic and in the general matrix of morality.

Another characteristic of the new look in programs for the teacher's major is the insistence that he learn to view knowledge as "fragile, dubitable," rather than dogmatic. He must perceive his scholarly task as *seeking* rather than *having* knowledge. For example, J. J. Schwab describes science "as a product of fluid enquiry" rather than as a "rhetoric of conclusions."[11] This perception of the dynamic rather than the static nature of academic fields of study is strongly represented among scientists. It is present but perhaps less emphasized in the concerns of humanists as they discuss the goals of the teacher's work in his major.

A final problem merits attention. It derives from the expectation that the teacher will develop into an autonomous and continuing learner in his subject field. He is called on to gain the competences needed to continue learning on his own, and to learn to *want* to continue. In brief, he should gain not only *skill* in learning but *love of learning*—and be able to communicate both of these to his students.

'Personal' Outcomes of Specialization for the Teacher

The study of a discipline should have personal consequences for the teacher far beyond those that relate directly to his subject field. This optimistic view of the general values of special education persists tenaciously in the writings of educators. In this view a discipline is to be learned as a study having attachments not only to one's field of study and to other fields of study but also to a wide range of personal and social problems faced by the teacher. He should study his major in such a

---

[11] "The Teaching of Science as Enquiry," in the *Inglis Lecture of 1962*. Cambridge: Harvard University Press.

way as to make his disciplinary learnings responsive, relevant, and transferable to his personal and social transactions, to the whole conduct of his life.

For example, the teacher is often seen stereotypically as intellectually impoverished, socially inept, sentimental rather than hard-headed, and often infantilized by association with children. There is enough truth in these half-truths to spur educators to seek in the outcomes of the teacher's major studies the remedies for such personal deficiencies.

For example, Conant hopes that the teacher's major will help him to become less timid in attacking other difficult problems and that he will be less likely "to accept dogma or to countenance nonsense on any subject."[12] Another educator, more enthusiastic than Conant, hopes that teachers will learn to think in disciplinary terms as part of their whole approach to living. (Why *they* should when so few other educated people do is not made clear.)

In addition, we may surely hope that the rigorous study of a discipline will contribute to the development of the teacher's concept of himself and to his professional identity. In this connection former U.S. Commissioner of Education S. N. McMurrin has said:

> We cannot avoid the impression that the average graduate of our professional schools of education is not especially proud of his own education . . . he often seems inclined to suspect that in some ways he has been short-changed, that those who have gone through letters or science . . . have fared better than he.

The truth of this statement can hardly be questioned. If so, then this sense of having been given a second-rate education may have a serious effect upon the teacher's perception of himself as a professional and as an educated person.

It is then perhaps permissible to speak of designing major programs for teachers that will contribute constructively to their perception of their own worth as teachers and as members of a society of scholars. Among some students this sense of af-

---

[12] *Op. cit.,* p. 106

112

filiation with scholars often seems to conflict with the sense of affiliation with the community of teachers, but this risk will have to be taken. There is good evidence that the associations of teachers are already strengthening their own attachments to disciplinary scholarship and thus are dealing with the problem.

In any event, the men and women who are engaged in the development of programs of majors for teachers will need to devise experiences through which the teacher may capitalize on his disciplinary learnings to extend them beyond subject matter boundaries, to sustain him in his personal and professional life.

The Heuristic Uses of a Major

The teacher's major must be resource to him in developing his classroom curriculum. No matter how detailed a school syllabus may be, the teacher still has to invent the curriculum anew in every class. This necessity for constant creation and re-creation of the curriculum derives from a multiplicity of circumstances: individual differences among pupils, intra-pupil changes, advances in the discipline itself, the changes in the school and its society, and more. The teacher must know his subject in such a fashion that it serves him as a heuristic resource on which he draws to invent the curriculum for his pupils.

The teacher is, in addition, constantly setting objectives for instruction. Some of these, it is true, arise from societally given goals, while others derive directly from the internal logic of the subject itself. In either case, the teacher has to reorganize his own disciplinary learnings constantly as he deploys and redeploys them in the service of his objectives.

For example, René Dubos speaks of "humanistic biology" as dealing with the "biological determinants . . . in manifestations of life that are most characteristically human, for example, ecstasy, logic, or simply the experience of happiness or despair."[13] If the teacher were called on to teach objectives relating to such an unusual and valuable topic, he would need to be able to retrieve from his study of biology the appropriate content.

---

[13] "Humanistic Biology," *The American Scholar*, Vol. 34, No. 2, Spring, 1965, p. 179.

Such a task would probably be impossible for most teachers unless their major collegiate courses had prepared them for it or had helped them to gain the general resources and the flexibility to deal with novel problems in their field.

But even in dealing with familiar topics, the teachers need to have ready access to a great range of curricular resources. They need to devise content appropriate, for example, to the instruction of culturally deprived pupils, or "thing-oriented" or "people-oriented" pupils, or for those who are committed to vocations. Such requirements force them to select and reorganize the content of their subject. To do so competently they have to be disciplined to select important content and to ask important questions about it. And it is clear that too many teachers take important content and ask trivial questions of it—or waste the pupils' time entirely by selecting trivial content.

The teacher's study of his discipline must also prepare him to make decisions about what is *not* appropriate for him to teach. Why have so many English teachers never learned that they are not competent to deal technically with concepts of social class or with Oedipus complexes? Why do so many spinster teachers feel they are fully qualified to teach about sex education and marriage problems? In sum, why do so many teachers meddle with ideas and issues they are *not* qualified to deal with? A good part of the answer is that they have never in the study of their discipline learned not to trespass beyond the boundaries of their expertise and competence. Yet this kind of necessary scholarly humility is undoubtedly best learned through the study of a discipline.

Perhaps the teacher most needs to be a virtuoso in the deployment of content when he acts as an educational decision-maker. Up until fairly recently, teachers have operated in their classrooms with completely inadequate feedback about their pupils' progress, their learning difficulties, their attitudes toward the content, the teacher, and the methods of instruction. But these feedback and data processing systems are rapidly being developed today. At one experimental public school (the Oakleaf School, Baldwin-Whitehall, Pennsylvania) the teachers of mathematics, for example, are getting almost minute-by-minute data about their pupils' progress and their learning problems. They receive a continual stream of information about precisely where the pupil is in an ordered, detailed curriculum stated in behavioral terms. If a pupil falters in a certain set of multiplication problems, for example, the teacher may be informed not only of this fact but also that the pupil has difficulty in knowing *when* to multiply, or that he has mastery of one-digit numbers but makes errors with two-digit numbers, or that he can perform the pencil and paper operations but cannot *verbally* describe what he is doing and why. The teacher also knows when a pupil has mastered one sequence of the curriculum and somehow or other, by insight or transfer, is able to demonstrate that he has mastery of the next sequence. This kind of information is available for each sub-topic of a study, so that each pupil's learning status is plotted in relation, for example, to the sequences in numeration, direct measurement, addition, subtraction, and so on. In addition, the teachers have access to a wide variety of curricular materials and instructional aids. Given all this knowledge about each pupil, what kind of prescriptions do the teachers write for them? Do they mechanically assign the next three pages or the next three behavioral goals if the pupil demonstrates mastery? Or can they rather invent new materials for the pupil who is ready to take a long leap forward? Can they devise a new curriculum for the pupil who is capable of mastering the required work and is motivated to carry out independent study, or for the one who is ready to go ahead with self-initiated explorations of unusual problems, or for the one who demonstrates a potential for creativity? A large part of the answer to such questions about the teacher's responsiveness to individual differences depends on the depth and scope of his mastery of the subject and upon the flexibility and creativity with which he can focus his resources upon the tasks of diagnosing and prescribing for his pupils. In brief, upon the heuristic value of his major to him as a classroom decision-maker.

'Process Learnings' and the Collegiate Major

If "structures" constitute the systemic, organizational essence of a discipline, then "process learnings" are the "spin-offs."

That is, process learnings are the incidental, often unanticipated outcomes of study. They include both cognitive and affective changes accompanying the acquisition of disciplinary learnings. The process outcomes may at times be of *more* importance than the primary learnings, as, for example, if in the process of learning to read a child also learns to hate reading, or if he develops an incapacitating emotional block to reading. In many instances, the process learnings help determine the associations, extensions, applicability, and transfer value of the pupils' formal learnings. They constitute a sphere of resonance, of the connotations rather than of the denotations of scholarly learning.

Process learnings would, for example, include what the anthropologist Jules Henry has called "learning docility or giving teacher what she wants," even if what she wants if patently wrong. Glenn Heathers speaks of the important process goals of self-evaluation with a criterion of mastery, and of problem-solving thinking, among others. And the examples may be multiplied: Some pupils learn Latin, others learn to be virtuosos in cheating by way of interlinear translations; still others learn to ask questions or not to ask questions; many learn to expect that their school learnings will not be relevant outside of class. Edwin H. Land, in the A. D. Little Memorial Lecture on the state of instruction at MIT (1957), writes that the freshmen enter college

> honest and honorable and full of ideas; that they come to the door of our universities with the dream of being [the faculty's] colleagues; that if we could provide them with intimate leadership there would be no discipline to which they would not subject themselves and no task so arduous in the pursuit of knowledge and science that they would not devote themselves fully to it. But if we imply, as I believe we do by our present attitude, that we do not have this kind of faith in them, then their strength wanes and they cannot believe the best of themselves.

In sum, says Land, they learn to distrust themselves. The system of tests and grades teaches them "never to get into a situation where they can be marked again." They learn to extend the period of their immaturity because they are treated like boys.

Bruner's essays on knowing constitute almost a primer on process outcomes:

> . . . learning to discover, to guess, to use intuition, sentiment, disciplined fantasy; to invent, to make new connections, to use art as a mode of knowing, to be committed to understanding rather than to rote, to respect the tools and materials of work. The individual must ultimately learn to go "beyond the cultural ways of his social world. . . to create his own version of the world, using that part of his cultural heritage he has made his own through education.[14]

It is quite clear that process learnings comprise some of the most important outcomes of education, but they are eclipsed at present by the attention educators are giving to the disciplinary reconstruction of the curriculum, and perhaps stunted by a widespread reluctance among some educators to advocate anything except narrowly defined intellectual development. Yet it is likely that ultimately the renaissance of the curriculum for our schools will *not* revolve around the reconstruction of formal disciplinary studies. If we are to have a new curriculum, it will have to be constructed around the fusion of disciplinary studies with conscious and systematic instruction for process learnings.

If this is true, then our teachers will have to learn about process learnings while they build up their competence in the field of their academic specialization. To do otherwise would be like studying society without reference to culture, or poetry without reference to connotation.

THE STATUS OF PROGRAMS OF SPECIALIZATION FOR TEACHERS

Many of the individuals and groups working on curriculum revisions for the schools are also concerned with the preparation of the teachers who will use the new materials. It may be useful to identify some of the characteristics of their recommendations for the teacher's program in his major. In the preparation of this overview I have sampled the work of a few representative

---

[14]*On Knowing: Essays for the Left Hand, op. cit.,* p. 116 *et passim.*

professional associations and nationally recognized spokesmen in this field.[15]

Perhaps the most frequently stressed recommendation is the injunction to avoid the attempt to "cover" the substantive knowledge in a field of study. Almost all such statements make direct reference to "structures" as a principal ingredient in the content of major programs and as the organizing theme in them. At Harvard, Fletcher Watson proposes however a "spread" of courses for science teachers rather than narrowly designed programs. He also recommends that the major be organized around those topics that can best be mastered through formal collegiate study, omitting those topics that the teacher can develop on his own through independent study and reading. If this is feasible, it seems like an eminently sensible idea, especially in view of the general expectation in almost every field that the teacher will have to systematically continue his education, both formally and informally, beyond the baccalaureate degree.

Several groups speak of gradations or levels of preparation. The Mathematical Association of America suggests five levels, corresponding to the requirements for teachers in elementary schools (K-6), junior high schools (7-9 or 10), high school (9-12), a fourth level for teachers of advanced programs in high school, junior college, and college freshman and sophomore years, and the fifth level for full-fledged teachers of college mathematics. The Illinois State-wide Curriculum Center recommends three levels of preparation for English teachers: "Minimal" (not recommended but prerequisite), "Good," and "Su-

---

[15] Reference was made to the writings of J. B. Conant and B. O. Smith ("generalists"); in the field of English, E. R. Steinberg, G. R. Carlsen, and the Illinois State-wide Curriculum Center for Preparation of Secondary School Teachers of English; P. S. Jones, summarizing recommendations of the Panel on Teacher Training of The Committee on the Undergraduate Program in Mathematics; E. Hocking, commenting on teacher education in modern foreign languages; F. Watson, on preparation for teaching the natural sciences; E. Klinckmann, on preparation for teaching biology (Biological Sciences Curriculum Study); R. F. Lefler, reviewing the work on the preparation of teachers of physics (Cooperative Committee on the Teaching of Science and Mathematics, National Association of State Directors of Teacher Education and Certification, and the American Association of Physics Teachers); R. L. Silber, on chemistry.

perior." Conant states his general recommendations in terms of credit hours: thirty-six for elementary teachers and forty-eight for secondary teachers.

The bland prescription of a "good, sound undergraduate major," defined only as the courses regularly taken by all the undergraduate majors, is notable by its absence. On the contrary, there is very substantial agreement that the major programs for teachers should include course work specially designed for them. However, it must be noted that specially designed programs for teachers leave several important questions to be answered. What will the college student who has taken the "regular" major have to do if he wants to teach? Or conversely, what will the graduate with the special major for teachers have to do if he wants to take a master's degree in his subject field? In this connection there is some hope that some of the best of the special programs for teachers may turn out to be equally appropriate as the regular major, or vice versa. So far, however, these questions are not receiving much attention in higher education.

As for the problem of the teacher's gaining competence in teaching for process learnings, several writers touch indirectly upon the desirability of teaching for these outcomes. For example, P. S. Jones enjoins the mathematics teacher to abandon rote learning for himself and rote teaching for his pupils. He also notes the need to teach for motivation. Erwin Steinberg comes closer to process goals when he writes of a major program for English teachers that will empower them to teach so that their pupils may understand themselves and their relation to the environment. He also touches upon the need to teach skills of evaluation, but it is not clear whether he refers to Heathers' "self-evaluation with a criterion of mastery" or to the evaluation of literature, although the latter seems more likely.

In any event, none of the educators concerned with teacher education approach the need to teach for process learnings with the insight, the elegance, and the conviction displayed by Bruner. As noted earlier, the implications and the importance of process learnings are not yet competing successfully with concerns about substantive learnings among the men and women who are designing programs of majors for teachers.

In discussions of the qualifications needed by the professors who are to offer the major work for teachers, there is very general agreement that these professors *should be drawn from the faculties in the arts and sciences* rather than from education. Two other important recommendations are occasionally made. The first is that these instructors be well informed about the schools and well versed in the kind of instruction offered in them. The second is that specialists in public school instruction should have a voice in setting up the programs of majors. It is hardly necessary to note first that both of these recommendations are easier said than done; second, that they are very likely to be neglected because men possessing all of these qualifications are difficult to find; and third, that failure to find and recruit such instructors will undoubtedly slow down both the process of improving the competence of teachers to deal with their content and the process of improving public education.

THE UNIVERSITY AND THE GUARANTEES OF QUALITY

How well are the universities and colleges meeting their institutional responsibility for safeguarding the quality of the teacher's major studies? Some colleges simply and straightforwardly decline to offer degree programs for teachers. For example, Princeton. This unqualified "No" has one great advantage—it keeps everybody honest. Other universities accept the responsibility and do their honest best to bring resources, sanctions, and talent to the task. For example, Harvard and Stanford. This unqualified "Yes" also has several great advantages. It openly announces the institution's commitment to students, profession, and the public, and it generates a substantial amount of healthy guilt about how badly the job is done. This kind of divine discontent helps to keep the faculties working hard for improvement.

But still other colleges and universities—perhaps the majority—say neither "Yes" nor "No." For example, Yale. And it is this halfway status that causes so much trouble. To be engaged in but not committed to a difficult task creates extreme stresses for scholars.

Some react by scapegoating. Fred Hechinger of the *New York Times* cites an article in the *American Journal of Physics*

120

reporting on two surveys of the views of physics professors about the physics programs in the schools and about the education of physics teachers. The evidence indicates that "many college physics professors and department chairmen" are making little use of the students' high school preparation in physics, acting as though even the "reformed" physics courses were a waste. "Some respondents even admitted that they were not familiar with the work of the Physical Science Study Committee . . ." Hechinger goes on to comment editorially:

> Among the most revealing college comments was that too little was being done by "educators" to improve the training of high school physics teachers. This criticism appears to ignore the fact that college physics departments rather than schools of education ought to assume major responsibility for the training of competent physics teachers.[16]

Another source of stress within college faculties is generated by the fact that today "the teachers in the schools for the masses must be prepared in institutions of higher education, the traditions of which are more aristocratic than equalitarian. . . ."[17] It is worth noting that the aristocracy operating here is intellectual rather than social. And as a result, this intellectually select group of professors and their college students tend to find themselves at greater and greater distances from many of the pupils in the schools, less and less able or ready to understand them. It is no accident that the professors of arts and sciences, reentering the arena of the public school curriculum, have heavily concentrated their work on college preparatory courses, advanced placement programs, and the like. When a university has clearly elected to focus its program on the preparation of teachers for academically adept pupils, life is made easier for the professors. But when the programs are intended to prepare teachers for the generality of schools, then the aristocratic tradition often operates to make the major programs less and less appropriate for such teachers.

What are some of the outcomes of the many discontinuities between the schools and the institutions in which teachers are

---

[16] *New York Times,* Sunday, August 22, 1965, p. E-9.

[17] Mason, *op. cit.,* p. 383.

prepared? How do the universities deal with such problems? The most common strategy is evasion. For example, some make a brave show of institution-wide commitment and then allow the programs for teachers to become emasculated at the departmental level. In a very real sense some universities suspend their criteria of scholarship at this point. The code that makes universities responsible to students, to professions, and to the public becomes inoperative when these universities offer programs for the preparation of teachers.

In other instances the school of education is made autonomous. As a result, it frequently becomes encapsulated and isolated from the arts and sciences mainstream. A common result is separate but not equal education for teachers. Or the university may make the best but most difficult decision: to establish the education of teachers as a central institutional obligation, to hold itself truly responsible for preparing teachers in the same sense that it is responsible for preparing doctors, lawyers, and scholars in the disciplines, and to commit to this task its full resources.

The State, the School, and the Guarantees of Quality

It is abundantly clear that both experienced and novice teachers are likely to find themselves needing additional study in their major fields after graduation, first, in order to improve their disciplinary competences and to maintain contact with developments in their special field, and second, to meet the idiosyncratic requirements of the pupils and the schools. It is in this phase of continuing education that the state and the local school system must set up the guarantees of quality.

The state cannot meet this responsibility merely by the enactment of regulations. Many states are already striking out far beyond this, providing services and professional and financial support for continuing education. They seek, in a word, to combine regulatory with persuasive action and substantive assistance to insure quality.

But beyond this point it is the local school system that must assume the principal responsibility for encouraging the teachers to continue their studies. It is here, on the job, that the science teacher with a major in chemistry may be called on to teach earth science, or space biology. Or the history teacher with a concentration in European and American studies may have to deal with the history of Asian and African nations. If the school neglects to carry out its responsibilities to promote the teachers' continuing education in the disciplines, then the burden falls entirely upon the individual teachers. And for many of them this burden is too heavy to carry alone.

The school further influences the direction of continuing education for its faculty in a subtle fashion that is often overlooked. This directive force makes itself felt when the school commits itself to grand and noble objectives but "pays off" heavily on the basis of pupils' scores on Regents examinations or departmental examinations or the like. For example, if the school affirms its commitment to teaching English as the improvement of thought, comprehension, and communication, and then uses tests that pay off largely for knowledge of the formal rules of a Latinized English grammar, both pupils and teacher are likely to focus their continuing studies on formal English grammar. It is easy to predict what teachers will tend to study if the school *verbally* commits itself to teaching for mastery of structures and *operationally* focuses on data, taxonomies, and formulas.

In this matter of the discrepancy between stated objectives and operating objectives, it has been noted that the teacher himself is likely to pledge allegiance to grand objectives and flesh them out with trivial or inappropriate content and methods. In brief, broadly defined grand objectives become precarious if they are not translated into appropriate behavioral outcomes. When the schools employ the grand objectives for cosmetic or camouflage effect, the teacher is quite likely to be seduced into focusing his major studies upon cosmetics and camouflage. The responsibility for guarding against such abuses for both pupils and teachers is in large part the school's.

Perhaps the most important task of the local school system is to encourage continuing study by establishing the conditions for professionalism in the schools. Without such conditions, for example, the faculty room in the high school is likely to be filled with barrack-room grumbling and time-killing gossip rather than with shop talk. In essence, "shop talk" here is a shorthand expression for a professional environment, for the support provided to the teacher in his continuing education by the companionship and colleagueship of a group of peers also engaged in improving their professional competences.

The school also needs to create the necessary professional environment by supporting and rewarding further study, by providing resources for innovation and research. Programs of local and regional workshops can contribute to continuing study if they are concerned with important learnings, rather than with gossip or anecdote. Provision of leave with pay is obviously a powerful help to the teacher who wants to study full-time.

Perhaps the most potentially productive (and most abused) method of stimulating continuing study by teachers is the provision of supervisory services for them. The clinical supervisor working in the classroom with the teacher is especially influential when he helps the teacher to become aware of patterns of strength and weakness in his teaching, when he turns the current of the teacher's thought to the relation of content and method to objectives.

In sum, the school exercises a strong influence upon the continuing special education of teachers both directly and indirectly. Directly by requiring it and by creating conditions of work supportive of it, i.e., by providing, financing, and rewarding continued study. Indirectly by stressing the necessity for congruence between its stated objectives and what actually goes on in the classrooms, through its testing and grading program, and through provision of supervisory help.

CONCLUSION

After having examined the problems and issues connected with the improvement of programs of academic majors for teachers, the balance sheet looks something like this. Our assets include, first, the fact that the deep concern about the quality of these programs is less and less expressed in fault finding and more and more in constructive ideas and action, especially among academicians. Second, the work already under way is developing out of a fairly clear conception of 1) the weaknesses of present practice, 2) the characteristics and outcomes desired of the new programs, and 3) the clear recognition of the mandate that the university, the state, and the school must assume responsibility for the quality of the program and for the continuing education of the teacher. In sum, we start with what seems to be an excellent—even elegant—conceptual foundation and framework.

The liabilities in our balance sheet are, in short, the familiar human difficulties of getting teachers, universities, states, school systems, and the public all mobilized to do what needs to be done. But this time the nation may do just that with the help of the U.S. Commissioner of Education and Lyndon Johnson, who together seem determined that education will shape up or ship out of the Great Society.

Discussion of the Cogan Paper

BELLACK: I am going to take just a few minutes to identify what seems to me to be one of the major issues posed for us in teacher education with reference to the teaching major or the academic major for the future teacher. Mr. Cogan states in his paper that to subscribe to the idea of a good, solid academic major for all prospective teachers is not to solve the problem; it is only to uncover its complexities. As he indicates, the tendency is to make the objectives of the school correspond to the objectives of collegiate disciplines. Thus when it comes to identification of majors for the future teachers, we tend to identify these majors in terms of the disciplines as formed in the universities and research centers. This approach is very clearly mirrored in the many task force reports that we have had in the various sciences—in biology, physics, and chemistry—and to some extent in the social sciences, particularly in economics and to some extent in history and geography.

Now whether or not the individual research disciplines are to be viewed as the most appropriate teaching majors for prospective teachers depends on one's conception of the curriculum they are to teach. For example, what shall be the academic teaching major of the primary teacher who will be responsible for instruction in most of the subjects included in the curriculum? How shall we conceive of the teaching major for the junior high school teacher who is preparing to teach "science"? Should he major in chemistry, or physics, or biology? Or would a broad-fields program that includes all three of these disciplines be more appropriate? What about the social studies teacher? Should he major in *one* of the social sciences in his training program?

It seems clear that questions such as these can be dealt with only in the context of what is to be taught in the elementary and secondary schools and how the teaching fields that comprise the curriculum are to be organized. Without some conception of the nature of the teaching fields to be included in the school's program and how these teaching fields are to be organized in an overall curriculum design, it is difficult indeed to discuss the question of what the teaching majors of the prospective teachers should be. This means that those who plan the programs of teacher education ought to give attention to the work of educational theorists (like Philip Phenix in his *Realms of Meaning*) who have made proposals regarding alternative ways in which knowledge in various dimensions might be organized for pedagogical purposes.

BOYAN: As Mr. Bellack was speaking I began to wonder whether it might not be possible to view this problem in somewhat the same way that Harry Broudy tried to help us with the foundations this morning. It may not be a matter of "either-or" but of placing *both* of these ideas on some kind of a continuum, leading to a notion of applicability. In this way we then might be able to capitalize on the power of both the possibilities Mr. Bellack is talking about. I have some doubts that we will ever really be able to shape the academic majors in all institutions in such a way that they in turn approximate the content as it seems appropriate to teach it in the schools. Traditionally, we have expected the methods professor, or the curriculum and instruction professor (as we call him here at Stanford), to serve basically as the translator, the one who helps the potential teacher, the teacher-candidate, to translate the content he has learned in one setting into applicability in another setting. Perhaps this means then that we need much more powerful developments in the so-called methods and C and I areas along the lines of Mr. Phenix's approach, the Illinois approach, and so on, so that we can really capitalize on the one kind of power which is generated from one kind of program and blend it in and add to it another kind of power that is developed by people who have a particular commitment to, and more than an intuitive systematic familiarity in, the domain where the knowledge is to be applied. I think in a sense this is *the* professional task.

BELLACK: We also ought to have our eyes on the way in which we think the curriculum ought to be organized for teaching purposes. For example, Jerome Bruner now is involved in the development of a unified social studies program at Educational Services Incorporated. The social studies program is not organized around traditional disciplines in the social sciences; rather, the content of the proposed course is Man. Three questions recur throughout: What is human about human beings? How did they get that way? How can they be made more so? When we talk about developing teaching majors we ought to have proposals such as this one in mind, together with the proposals from the universities for requirements of a major in economics, sociology, etc.

STONE: I think whether we can ever get our academic colleagues to design collegiate curriculums that truly relate to the curriculums of the schools is an interesting academic question, but it has its practical side too. We in California have been going through the throes of this problem, particularly as it relates to the elementary school teacher.

In 1961 when new legislation governing credentialling of California teachers was passed (the so-called Fisher Bill), it required that all teachers, including elementary school teachers (where I think we have more of a problem than we do at the secondary level), should major in an academic subject-matter area. Presumably, the theory behind this idea was that intensive study of an academic discipline of whatever kind provides in and of itself certain values by way of knowing something well which gives one confidence to go ahead and teach it; by having studied something thoroughly one learns the technique and the rationale and the methodology of the discipline. So if you have to teach other disciplines when you get into teaching, you have the know-how to attack them and can go on and learn them on your own. This was the theory.

Now, as a result of legislation that was just passed in Sacramento this summer we have a new concept which says that elementary school teachers should major only in subjects which are commonly taught in the elementary school. And, similarly, secondary teachers should major only in subjects which are commonly taught in the secondary school. Now, presumably, this means that our academic curriculum should be geared to the elementary school program, on the one hand, for elementary candidates, and to the secondary school program, on the other hand, for secondary candidates. And then we suddenly wonder what has happened to the wonderful disciplines many of our elementary candidates are majoring in: psychology, anthropology, sociology, political science, and philosophy—not subjects commonly taught *per se* in the elementary school and therefore not fitting preparation for elementary school teachers. So you see, we're hung up with one conception while practicing another one; so this is not only an academic discussion that we're concerned with here, but one with a lot of practical applications. In California we're not sure where we really are on this issue. And yet we're in the daily business of trying to guide prospective teachers. What do you do?

BARNES: Some curriculum makers of course are inclined to abandon the conventional disciplines. They prefer a "problems approach" which deals with current issues and questions. They use content to solve real questions without regard to the subject fields.

BELLACK: Well, my impression is that Mr. Bruner is not very much interested in practical problems of that kind but rather he is interested in development of a new structure of knowledge in the social sciences that might not correspond to sociology, political science, etc. As a matter of fact, his group says so rather specifically in their initial proposal for the social studies curriculum. They are still interested in teaching the *structure* of the discipline but the discipline is not, they say, economics, sociology, etc., but a unified notion of the social sciences. And they are developing a new structure composed of concepts from a variety of disciplines.

BARNES: McCutchins wrote an article perhaps two or three years ago in which he argued that the social studies as we think of them in the public school curriculum are themselves a discipline or are becoming a discipline.

BUSH: I have nothing to contribute at this time, but it interests me to observe that the members of ESI, fathered by a physicist, could not in the early stages get together in the field of the sciences. For example, the PSSC couldn't get chemistry and physics together. They now intend apparently to launch into an area outside of their competence and attempt to bring it together. I am not hopeful about their success.

STONE: The difference is, Mr. Bush, that I can come down here and be an expert but when I go 25 miles up the highway I'm nothing—same idea.

MORK: This bears on an interesting point that two or three people have made today, namely, that one of the outcomes of thorough study of any field should be the development of an academic modesty in that field. It hasn't been quite expressed that way but this is what has been inferred. I think we're all acquainted with the person who goes abroad and comes home an expert in everyone else's field. He is willing to make sweeping pronouncements about all fields except his own, because in his own he is aware of the problems and the difficulties and he's very cautious about saying anything. But he knows everything about all the other fields. And I suspect this is why these fellows are not reluctant at all to reorganize the social studies. They don't know very much about that area!

STONE: By implication, maybe we should reorganize the sciences while we're at it.

COGAN: You don't *have* to reorganize the sciences, since the first volume of the Physical Science Study Committee is entitled "The Universe."

BOYAN: Mr. Bush, now that we've identified the "bad guy" and we're beating him, maybe we could bury him and come back to the problem.

DAVIES: I wonder if any of you share the impression I have that not very many people in professional schools of education are spending very much time thinking about, talking about, or making recommendations about the nature of academic preparation for the prospective teacher. It seems to me that we've abdicated responsibility. We're leaving it up to the California legislature or somebody else to make decisions for us.

STONE: Douglas Minnis [in audience], can you tell us what's going on in the languages?

MINNIS: Well, first of all, let me say that perhaps the reason not too much attention is being paid to the academic major in general education so far is a little bit like the king's clothes: If somebody looks at the problem too closely, it makes sense that he'll find a considerable amount of farce there. But we have had some rather good fortune in the last year while working in a new context in particular subject-matter fields. We've tried both social studies and English on an in-service basis, which takes us out of the categories we have so well defined at the university, and find that we must get out our pencils and take notes or be afraid to admit our ignorance. We also have been able to utilize a rather broad region as a basis for this, so we now have 22 counties cooperating in revising the English curriculum, a prototype which we hope will be adopted by the state. It's interesting that in this context professors of English are quite willing to accept our expertise and we are more able to accept theirs—a little bit of application to theory.

BROUDY: As I listen to this, it seems to me the whole issue of whether teaching is a professional field or not comes up again. There is such a thing as general collegiate education, so-called liberal education, and I can't see much merit in any argument for transferring the jurisdiction over it from the liberal arts college. If after two thousand years they don't know how to design and administer general undergraduate education, then the prognosis for anyone else doing it better is not good. And I think we have no business telling liberal arts colleges what general education is. We can tell them as professionals where they make mistakes in teaching it, but institutionally they write the ticket. I have argued elsewhere that a teacher needs general education no more and no less than any human being. Now, it may very well be that to get a good general education one ought to have a major. This is not a professional question. The professional question is this: You want to be a teacher of this specialty. What, over and above your general education in various disciplines, do you need to work at this specialty?

There's no *a priori* answer to this. It may require the major. It may require survey courses. It may require interdisciplinary study. For example: Suppose we decided that an elementary science teacher ought to know how to construct laboratory apparatus. We might send her to the engineering school to learn how to construct apparatus or to a machine shop; or we might set up our own course. The question is not where it's done, but who says that it is to be done. No medical school would permit any liberal arts college to write the pre-medical ticket. No law school is letting anyone else write the pre-law special-content ticket. Should a supervisor of guidance have a major in logic or psychology? Only the college that prepares specialists in guidance knows what he needs over and above general education. While I agree with Mr. Cogan's substantive analysis of the situation, I think the situation is symptomatic of a wavering jurisdiction, of our loss of confidence in knowing what it takes to work in our field. Of course, if we don't know, then the thing to do is to ask advice from one who does. But if we don't know, then again we have no right to make believe that we're running professional schools. We're running service departments for the liberal arts college which may have graduates who want to teach.

DAVIES: Do we educate teachers in the disciplines and make the public school curriculum look like the disciplines, or do we devise a new kind of interdisciplinary general education for the universal study of teachers? Some say that the reason we haven't done the latter is that we're not professional. It strikes me that there may be another reason why we haven't done it: It's too hard to do.

BROUDY: Oh, but that's no reason.

COGAN: Oh, but it *is* a reason; we don't do anything unless we can do it well. That is, we expect to create the equivalent of a discipline just as you're expecting Bruner to create a discipline according to . . .

BROUDY: I'm not. This is an extremely unoriginal organization, if you know the history of social studies, but . . .

COGAN: I'm making no plea for the disciplines, but if we're going to teach something other than the disciplines, we've had previous attempts to do so. For example, general education in the colleges or interdisciplinary education in the school curriculum. One thing I know deep in my bones: If we're going to teach something new we had better know it, organize it in depth, give it a conceptual frame, make it something that does bear intellectual probing, that does reward study. We just can't do it in a half-baked manner. And this is one of the reasons, I think, why educators are standing back a little bit from the whole question of the special education of teachers: They are not prepared with a substitute.

BROUDY: I think the educator has been beaten over the head, scared to death by a lot of things, but let me give an example. What should a teacher of secondary English literature study in English over and above general education? Let's grant that whatever English she happened to have, even if she had a major, may not be enough. Now I submit that this is a professional question, but it is one on which the discipline scholar can advise. It is not obvious that taking another major or even a master's in English literature answers the question. For example, what is the role of Middle English in teaching high school English? How much Middle English should one study? How much philology? Now *a priori*, anything that's English presumably would have some relationship to the teaching of English. What a teacher of English needs in order to maneuver easily in a Shakespeare class is not simply a major in English literature or philology. Who makes that decision? I would like to think that the people at the university level who prepare English teachers are themselves able to know, and if they don't know they should collaborate with professors of English. But this is quite different from saying, "Go take another major," which is exactly what we've been urged to say.

BUSH: Who should make the decision? It should be a cooperative one by the scholars in the disciplines in the universities, the educators who are concerned with the preparation of teachers, and those who are teaching in schools at the particular level where instruction is going to be given. Unless these three groups participate the decision is likely to be a bad one. I think we're making genuine progress in having elementary and secondary school teachers of mathematics get together with the college and university teachers and educationists of the various methodological and foundational disciplines to hammer out a curriculum. They are not looking at it just as elementary mathematics, for example; they're looking at it all the way along. The biologists are better off than the physicists, it seems to me, because the bioloigsts have been looking at a curriculum all the way from the elementary school through the university. As we move away from mathematics, foreign languages, and English and get into the sciences, things become a little more complicated. Then you get into the social field and the humanistic field and they get still more complicated. But the fact of more complications does not relieve us of the necessity of working on the basis we found to work for the simpler situation.

BROUDY: Who's running the show on the collaboration?

BUSH: Where the power and logic of the ideas reside. The ultimate responsibility, or let's say the leadership, rests with the people who are engaged in the teacher education programs—the science educator, the mathematics educator. There is no question in my mind about that. The matter is one for *professional* decision. Do you agree?

BROUDY: Absolutely. Yes.

ADJOURNMENT

Chapter V

Building School-University Relations in Teacher Education

MELVIN W. BARNES
Superintendent of Schools
Portland, Oregon

First, a word of caution. You should be aware that I speak as a garden-variety practitioner in a public school system. It just might be that teacher education is not a subject on which I am licensed to preach. Moreover, I can not forget that I am speaking to an audience which includes many professors and graduate students. This is a disquieting thought, and it suggests a show card that hung in a New York subway with a message for prospective school dropouts. The card pictured a wretched misfit and carried the caption, "I quit school in fifth grade." Under it someone had pencilled, "You was a smart kid. I staid on thru collidge."

It is only right to acknowledge that you who have stayed on are contributing much more significantly to teacher education than we who have dropped out. My thesis will be, however, that we have business to do together.

Teacher education needs help. Anyone surveying the educational scene today is forced to conclude that teacher education is not found in the *avant garde* of innovation. In contrast to the ferment and experimentation observable elsewhere, for example in pre-schools and community college, neither pre-service nor in-service programs for teachers are among the front-runners. In my judgment the most serious of the prevailing ailments are directly traceable to weak relationships between schools and universities. In listing a few, I shall not attempt to catalogue many shortcomings but rather to identify some of the most relevant, and incidentally, to support my belief that when it comes to creative innovation, teacher education is not where the action is.

If my conclusions hold water, then teacher education may well be the most strategic target for the continuing nationwide attack on the problem of improving schools.

SOME SOFT SPOTS

1. *Generally speaking, schools and universities are failing to pull together in the interest of teacher education.*

Two years ago a researcher who called at some forty university campuses to study the education of teachers reported that he had found appallingly few instances of substantial school-university cooperation. For example, he says that in the training of supervising teachers he could find little going on that was worth noting, despite the fact that almost everybody acclaimed the supervising teacher as the key to the whole process.[1]

A science educator in an Eastern university, on sabbatical leave this year, is visiting numerous teacher education programs. The gist of his report is that genuine school-university cooperation nowadays is hard to find. As a typical example, he mentions a university staff who indicate a readiness to discuss problems with neighboring school systems but who find the school people indifferent.

Another researcher of my acquaintance is handling a countrywide project to train mathematics teachers. He speaks of the rare cases of truly mutual reinforcement to be found between schools and universities. From his experience in various states, he describes as common situations where the superintendent of schools is the barrier to joint effort; where the dean of a school of education stands in the way; or where cooperation is thwarted in the mathematics faculty of the college.

Inquiries I have made lead to the conclusion that examples

---

[1] William Ward and John Suttle, "The Oregon Program for the Preparation of Supervising Teachers." Salem, Oregon: State Department of Education, p. 1. (Undated mimeo publication)

of close teamwork between schools and universities are few and far between.

2. *The initial teaching experience is a gold mine of opportunity that is by no means adequately exploited.*

Unquestionably, the practical, down-to-earth experience provided by student-teaching pays off. Several years ago I conducted a study with some sixty beginning teachers. In April, at the three-quarter mark in the school year, I invited these new teachers to help me appraise the different parts of their preparation programs now that they had completed several months on their first job. In the process, they answered a questionnaire and assembled for small group interviews.

The one compelling conclusion was that, with all its shortcomings, the student-teaching experience stood alone as the most significant part of their preparation. From firsthand acquaintance I knew that their student-teaching had been ordinary "mine run." For them, as for most, the college supervisors merely had sought out classroom teachers willing to accommodate students. There had been no thought of giving the supervising teachers special training for inducting fledgling teachers. They had simply muddled through. Under such circumstances, if the outcome was as good as the beginners believed, one can only contemplate how telling the impact might have been with a genuinely thoughtful and creative use of supervisory strategies and techniques.

An *NEA Journal* article dealing with this problem quotes a new teacher as saying, ". . . I was literally abandoned to the isolation of my own classroom. . . . Supervision was infrequent and brief, and evaluation of my teaching was seldom very accurate or helpful. Only once did I have a chance to discuss the observations of my supervisor."[2]

I do not believe that this experience is unusual. I know of situations where a supervisor of student teachers has responsibility for as many as forty students placed in widely scattered schools.

---

[2]Vern B. Archer, Roy A. Edelfelt, and Herbert Hite, "Point Points the Way," *NEA Journal,* Vol. 54, No. 7, October, 1965, p. 29.

3. There is too much "slippage" between theory and practice.

It is a common experience for students in preparation programs to become sharply aware that their theoretical instruction is divorced from reality.

Recently I had a conversation with a man who reported that his wife was taking college courses preparing to teach and was unhappy with her instruction because it seemed to bear so little relation to real-life teaching. Finally she took a day to visit school classrooms in action. From this contact with actual teaching she quickly caught a new relevance between her campus study and the real world of the classroom.

Those of us who have worked with new teachers know well enough that talking about an imaginary situation is nothing like dealing with one that really exists for us. In pre-school conferences, for example, you can discuss the inevitable discipline problems with the beginning teachers and they seem to understand. Six weeks later you meet them again. Having got their feet wet, they are eager for help with the perplexing problems of pupil control. The stock question is: "Why didn't somebody tell us?" This should be no surprise in view of what we know of the dependence of perception upon the perceiver's own experience.

In another *NEA Journal* article, a study of 300 beginning teachers is reported. The author says, "Beginners repeatedly expressed the conviction that [education] courses are too theoretical and lacking in practical application." Again, he states, "There is a distressing gap between what is taught in the education courses and the real world of teaching."[3]

This is an old chestnut. The loss of touch with reality is an occupational hazard for the researcher and the theoretician. However, we do not want to deal them out of the teacher education enterprise; we want to build in genuine experience in learning to teach.

Today, despite active efforts to promote the dissemination of ideas, teacher preparation programs seem extraordinarily con-

---

[3]Lawrence A. Lemons, "Education Courses," *NEA Journal*, Vol. 54, No. 7, October, 1965, p. 26.

servative. Consequently, they often fail to respond to curricular reform going on in the elementary and secondary schools. Moreover, both pre-service and in-service work may consist largely of gathering credits in courses taught by professors who themselves lag in their professional growth.

As evidence, may I cite a recent study which revealed that many professors of physics in colleges have not even heard of the PSSC physics course.[4] Regrettable and shocking as this seems to me, when I mentioned the findings of this study to a physicist of my acquaintance, he was not in the least surprised.

4. *The process lacks continuity.*

Pre-service and in-service "levels" of teacher education are separated by a gulf that is easy to see but difficult to close. Dr. Boyan, in a paper presented at the White House Conference on Education, said, "Lines of demarcation between pre-service preparation and initial employment require softening and blurring so that the latter is treated by design as a continuation of pre-service training."[5]

This is sound doctrine. In the business of educating teachers, public school administrators, teacher educators, and professors in the academic departments operate like independent entrepreneurs. This state of affairs interferes with communication and hinders the joint effort that might be put forward for the sake of sound teacher training. It is strange that we who profess such devotion to the principle of continuity in teaching and learning should so flagrantly violate this principle in the actual education of teachers.

This "splendid isolation" that leaves us in the schools to stick to our knitting and those in the universities to attend to their tasks suggests an old Marx brothers movie in which Groucho plays a lawyer in an office that is infested with houseflies. He explains, "We have a working arrangement with them. They don't practice law and we don't climb the walls."

[4]John W. Renner, Robert J. Whitaker, and Leticia B. Bautista, "Is High School Physics a 'Waste' for College Preparation?" *American Journal of Physics*, Vol. 33, No. 8, August, 1965, pp. 618-24.

[5]Norman J. Boyan, "Teacher Education," Consultants' Papers, The White House Conference on Education, Vol. 1, July, 1965, p. 30.

Whatever the reasons, we are not working well in the double harness and consequently the processes of teacher education are plagued by discontinuities.

5. *Methodology is underdeveloped and in disrepute.*

B. F. Skinner says, "The most widely publicized efforts to improve education show an extraordinary neglect of method. Learning and teaching are not analyzed, and almost no effort is made to improve teaching as such." He further comments, "It is also true that educational method has not been brought to . . . attention in a favorable light. Pedagogy is not a prestigious word."[6]

The study of beginning teachers cited above reported: "Interviewees generally condemned general methods classes . . . ; the chief criticism of methods courses seemed to be that they saw little connection between them and what goes on in the classroom."[7]

Professional performance requires more than subject-matter competence. A good teacher possesses skills and is able to use them artfully. Often a repertoire of techniques seems to be the chief difference between the successful teacher and the one who fails. Moreover, only through methodology can some of the more important goals of education be attained. This is true of almost all of the intellectual process goals as represented, for example, in the cognitive domain of Bloom's taxonomy.[8]

However, formal methods courses are often ineffective because they are highly abstract or swamped in generalities. Despite this judgment, we should argue for more instruction in methods, not less, under a truly cooperative partnership between the university and the school. Its purpose should be to analyze processes of learning and teaching in the setting of the teacher education program.

So much for the once-over-lightly of some apparent weak-

---

[6] B. F. Skinner, "Why Teachers Fail," *Saturday Review*, October 16, 1965, p. 80.

[7] Lemons, *op. cit.*, p. 26.

[8] Benjamin Bloom (ed.), *Taxonomy of Educational Objectives, Handbook I, Cognitive Domain.* New York: David McKay, 1956.

nesses in teacher education. Before this recital of infirmities assumes more of the character of a jeremiad, it is time to call a halt. Identifying ailments is a rather dismal business, and the above list presents some formidable problems. I believe, however, that all of the shortcomings are largely remediable if schools and universities will get together in an earnest effort to create realistic teacher education experiences for their students and initial practitioners.

The Teachers We Want

Before turning to the question of what changes are in order, I should like to take a moment to state a brief article of belief about preparation for teaching.

First, we assume that teachers ought to be educated. To challenge the curiosity and cultivate the intellect of learners, teachers need to possess knowledge and to know how to think. They must be masters of what they teach and able to move within their special disciplines with a measure of ease and assurance. Nothing substitutes for subject-matter competence, rigorously developed and conscientiously kept current. We can not compromise with teachers who present a spectacle of the blind leading the blind. Moreover, a teacher's preparation goes far beyond the subject matter to be taught. There is a substantial body of knowledge about education which belongs in the intellectual equipment of the professional person. He should know and understand it as one prerequisite to professional stature and status. Education is a discipline in itself.

Second, the trained teacher must also have a set of values, a philosophy relating to the purposes of teaching that will serve to guide and stabilize him in evaluating his own performance as well as that which he sees others saying and doing.

Third, the teacher must be schooled in the basic science of teaching. He should know the techniques of his profession and their appropriate uses. I believe it is safe to say that universities and colleges do better in giving liberal education than in developing professional skills. Infinitely more care and effort have gone into the former. Some teacher educators even doubt the value of methodology. As I heard one say recently, "If you are well educated and can talk, you can teach."

Fourth, a teacher must bring certain attitudes to his task. Unquestionably, the teacher's understanding of himself, as a means to understanding his students and of creating wholesome attitudes toward them, is by no means the least of his preparation for the classroom.

Our commitment to the importance of the knowledge, skills, and dispositions required to produce genuinely educated and trained teachers justifies our demand for intensive, systematic, and professional preparation of the first order of quality. To aim for anything less is to write off the teacher as essentially a functionary in a bureaucratic system.

I should like to turn now to four examples of school-university cooperation that happen to fall within the range of my experience and which may serve to illustrate some possibilities. This is a realm in which no one dare lay claim to final answers. There may not be any.

EXAMPLES OF PROMISING PARTNERSHIPS

Metropolitan Portland contains a number of higher education institutions, some ten of which are actively engaged in producing teachers. These institutions rely upon our school district, as well as our neighbors, to provide the laboratory in which prospective teachers get their introduction to classroom reality. This is an opportunity that we are learning to exploit.

The Clinical Professor

Several of our staff members hold "clinical professorships," with appointments in both our school system and Reed College or Portland State College. Such persons wear two hats, are on two payrolls, have two offices, teach in two institutions, and are accorded academic status in both.

You recognize here the influence of Morris Cogan, after whose work in supervision we have patterned some of our efforts. Several of our staff members have had the benefit of summer experiences at the University of Pittsburgh as well as in training programs Cogan has conducted in our state. In addition, Flanders, Amidon, Bantel, Taba, and Hughes are among those who have been working with us in developing patterns of partnership between school and university. In this venture, the assistance of the Oregon State Department of Education should be acknowledged. With a grant from the Ford Foundation, the department is providing some resources for development in teacher education.

Conant gives Robert Bush credit for creating the term "clinical professor."[9]

Following Bush, Conant, and Cogan, we call our teacher-professors "clinical professors." This year we have four. As would be expected, not all work exactly alike. There are variations in our several programs for interns and student-teachers.

The clinical supervision program serves several important purposes. It fosters continuity between pre-service and in-service experience, trains supervising teachers, spotlights the interaction between the supervisor and the intern or student-teacher, stresses the initial teaching experience as the golden opportunity for learning methodology, builds a corps of trained supervising teachers, and inevitably marries theory to practice. It is the best instrumentality we know to connect the school with the campus.

The clinical professor is recruited from the ranks of the public school staff. On campus, where he maintains office hours and teaches, he teams up with other professors who prepare teachers, both in education and in the academic branches of the institution. He assists in seminars for interns and student-teachers. He is the college supervisor of student-teachers.

In the schools, where he spends most of his time, the clinical professor continues to work as a faculty member in close touch with his associates, especially those who serve as supervising teachers in charge of the induction of the student-teachers or interns who are in contact with pupils.

The presence of clinical professors in our schools is resulting in increased numbers of teachers who want to supervise beginners, and our growing corps of supervising teachers is improving in competence, both as teachers and supervisors. Mainly, we are finding it possible to move forward on two

[9] James B. Conant, *The Education of American Teachers*. New York: McGraw Hill, 1963, p. 142.

fronts. First, we have tools for examining the interaction between supervising teacher and initial practitioner. In education this field is a sort of no-man's-land. A recent article by Blumberg and Amidon had this to say: "When supervisor and teacher confront each other, the former communicates various observations and generally makes his assistance available. But the manner in which the supervisor conducts himself and the information he attempts to transmit are elements crucial to the outcome of the conference.

"In view of the obvious importance of the supervisor in supervisor-teacher interaction, the paucity of research on the supervisory conference is surprising."[10]

Second, in investigating teacher-pupil behavior, we are encountering anew the question of what teaching is. This is pay dirt. It is hard to explain the prevailing neglect of analytical study of learning and teaching processes. Skinner points out that college teaching is not taught at all. He says, "The beginning [college] teacher receives no professional preparation. He usually begins to teach simply as he himself has been taught." Of the grade school and high school teacher, Skinner goes on to say, "Certain trade skills and rules of thumb are passed along, but the young teacher's own experience is to be the magic source of improvement."[11]

Certainly we can do better than to leave largely to chance both the skills learned in teaching teachers and those employed in teaching pupils.

Portland High School Curriculum Study

Several years ago the Portland Public Schools requested and received a Ford Foundation grant of $375,000 to support curriculum revision in the twelve high schools. The study paid for an extensive inquiry not only into college preparation but also into problems of continuity between high school and college. This was an almost unique instance in which a school system

---

[10] Arthur Blumberg and Edmund Amidon, "Teacher Perceptions of Supervisor-Teacher Interaction," *Administrator's Notebook*, Vol. XIV, No. 1, September, 1965.

[11] Skinner, *op. cit.*, p. 80.

approached nine neighboring colleges and universities, which receive 85 per cent of its high school graduates, with an invitation to a joint study of secondary education in the continuum from grade nine through college graduation. Ensuing developments brought together hundreds of professors and classroom teachers for extended periods of curriculum work. The plans of the initial study submitted in 1960 have been implemented on schedule, with the result that a continuing close relationship exists between the school system and the colleges and universities. Our experience supports the statement of Dr. Hanna, "No school can possibly design an adequate . . . program without intimate and continuous partnership of the professional school teacher and of the academic scholar."[12]

As would be expected, this study paved the way for other cooperative arrangements and relationships. Supervisors and teachers frequently say that, because of acquaintances formed in the conduct of the study, they freely confer with geographers, historians, scientists, and other scholars about specific teaching problems and also topics of general academic interest.

Carnegie Professional Growth Program

In-service education offers a solid opportunity for cooperation between schools and universities. Spurred by the massive curriculum projects that are radically transforming school curricula, in-service programs are sure to grow rather than decline. For better or for worse, we have struck our tents and have moved into new territory. The only way the changes can reach the practitioner is through in-service education.

Both the public schools and the colleges have a great stake in this. In one sense, the colleges are better equipped to meet in-service needs than are school districts, because it is part of the business of college professors to study and keep abreast of changes in their fields, and they normally can devote more time to this than can public school personnel. At the same time, public school people are in a better position to say which innovations hold the greatest promise in view of the conditions that exist

---

[12]Paul R. Hanna, "Mounting a National Effort in the Social Studies," *National Elementary Principal,* Vol. XLII, No. 6, May, 1963, p. 46.

in their districts—conditions which may include capabilities of the teaching staff, objectives of the local board of education, and the practicality of what is proposed. It seems obvious, therefore, that in-service education should be a joint concern and endeavor.

The Portland School District, through a grant from the Carnegie Corporation of New York, is attempting to build a prototype in-service education program in which the cooperation of the school district and the local state college is a prime element. To date we have accomplished these things:

Portland State College reviews every in-service course produced and approves or disapproves the course and its instructor as a numbered offering of the college. Courses are submitted for approval to department heads outside the school of education or to the school of education, whichever is appropriate. Where the instructor of an in-service course is a Portland teacher, as is usually the case, the course is offered through the State Continuation Division and carries credit from the appropriate college or university. The teacher is, in effect, a college staff member, and the teaching of the course brings well-deserved recognition to that teacher.

In the Carnegie program, extensive use also is made of college and university personnel as consultants. Nineteen committees of teachers and supervisors will meet this year to determine in-service needs in all areas of instruction and at all grade levels, and a college consultant will meet with each of them. The role of these consultants is advisory, and the final determination of need is in the hands of teachers and supervisors. These college consultants also will be on hand to advise and assist the classroom teachers who are selected to develop and teach the in-service courses.

In Oregon a new certification program gives each state college and university the right to determine what courses, within limits, should apply toward certification of a teacher. As a result, courses developed and taught by Portland teachers under the Carnegie program are often approved for certification. This means that an advisor may help a prospective teacher pick and choose from a much broader offering and thus bring about a closer fit than was formerly possible between the preparation of the teacher and the duties he will be required to perform in a classroom. I believe this kind of cooperation will contribute both to the improvement of in-service and pre-service education.

The Stanford-Marshall Project

Portland's Marshall High School employs the Stanford School Scheduling System, a technique commonly called "flexible scheduling." This was incorporated into the high school program in 1962. Drs. Bush, Allen, and Boyan are actively engaged with us in the research and development of the plan. The educational design incorporates a number of innovative ideas, including team teaching, large- and small-group instruction, independent study, flexible scheduling, new and extensive use of audio-visual resources, and use of para-professional personnel and resource centers. The Oregon Program, administered by the State Department of Education, is supporting the project, as it is the clinical professor program.

This "Marshall Plan" is noteworthy for the contribution it is making to the professional growth of the staff. This growth is coming about through deep engagement of the faculty in planning the school program, making the schedule, and in determining teacher assignments. The project has been the means of channeling to the school system novel ideas as well as the incentive to venture in new directions. For example, in its first summer, Portland teachers and administrators, besides some from other districts, had their initial experience in using a video-tape recorder, provided and handled by the Stanford staff to record and immediately play back live teaching situations for faculty observers to examine and evaluate. The attention which this workshop centered on learning and teaching proved that when process is assigned top priority, the gimmicks and paraphernalia of teaching assume appropriate subordinate roles.

This cooperative tie with Stanford has occasioned many visits by our staff to the Palo Alto campus for shorter or longer terms. The ideas are contagious. Presently four Portland high schools are moving along with experimental programs in which the Stanford faculty have an interest. Few weeks go by that do not see Stanford staff members in our schools following the

149

progress of the projects. Unquestionably, these continuing contacts directly affect staff development in the schools.

* * *

These four instances of cooperative action can make no pretense to the status of full-scale models of promising school-university partnerships. None of these can claim to be "it," but certain elements in them may be "ittish." They do respond in several ways to the soft spots that mark school-university relations.

Two of the most durable generalizations about public schools are (1) they should be improved, and (2) the key to better schools is better teaching. Certainly there is room for improvement. Cross-sectional surveys of classroom conditions prove that a great deal needs doing. Witness, for example, the ASCD publication, *The Junior High School We Saw—One Day in the Eighth Grade.*[13]

In this "shadow study," 102 skilled curriculum workers in ninety-eight schools in twenty-six states accompanied 102 junior high students in their classes for a typical day. The teaching these observers witnessed and reported fell far short of the best the profession knows how to provide.

Not only is there general belief that schools can be vastly improved but almost everybody is placing his bet on better teaching to do it. Clearly, no school can be better than its teachers. We would get better faster if schools and universities could relate responsibly and appropriately their mutual interests in the education of teachers. Now is the time to comb the new federal legislation in search of the means of support. Possibly Title IV funds can be expected to infuse teacher education with the required stimulus. At any rate, Washington seems to be waiting for local initiative to assert itself. Perhaps a move in this field, on a continental scale, should be the next order of business.

---

[13]ASCD Commision on Secondary Education. Washington, D.C.: The Association, 1964.

Discussion of the Barnes Paper

MORK: Yesterday I did this rather formally; today I'll do it informally. I want to say a few things about Superintendent Barnes' very fine talk. I was just asking him if he knows whether such a talk has been given at an AASA conference or meeting or convention. It ought to be. I'm going to write to Forrest Conner [executive secretary, American Association of School Administrators], who is a good friend of ours, and see if he in his omnipotence can't see that this topic is considered at AASA meetings; there's no doubt, as was well brought out in the talk, that we have a very important mutual stake in this. For those of us in teacher education this is our immediate responsibility; but our long-range responsibility is that of producing good teachers for schools, so this is where we come together. My own experience in this has been that the key to the situation is probably personnel hiring functionaries of our larger school systems. I know this is our experience and, Mr. Davies, you'll recall this in your work in Minneapolis which preceded mine: We get wonderful cooperation from the elementary and secondary personnel offices because they want our best teachers. If they want our best teachers they also want them to student-teach so that they can not only identify them but help to get them ready for the job.

To draw on your point of the mutual use of staff, an example would be a plan we're using this year. A girl who is on leave from the schools in the city where we're located is working as a coordinator of our elementary student-teaching program and has thus become intimately involved with all phases and aspects of student-teaching. Next year she will return to that city's school system and I am hoping that we can, after a time, do what you have done in the making of a joint appointment.

I'm sure that Phi Delta Kappa and Stanford make a real

contribution in bringing your talk into this symposium and getting this dimension of teacher education so clearly out into the open, Mr. Barnes. There are just a few things I'd like to add that we might also give some thought to. One of them is that the relationship between the college and the public school is clarified and enhanced if there is a contract for operation. We have these and they work very well. Mr. Davies, I think, helped to draw up these contracts at one time; they define the relationship between the public school system and the university. They're signed by representatives of the university board of regents and by representatives of the school board in the city involved. Beyond this, though, you need a set of agreements that are not necessarily drawn as a legal document to define areas of responsibility and authority. This is something which needs careful definition, because if there is any concern that the public school system has above all others, it is that the college or university may encroach on its responsibilities. It should always be made clear that a school system has the responsibility for the children in the classroom and the basic curriculum procedures and organization for the school. It is the responsibility of the college to be sure that it does not encroach on these or try to usurp any of the school's prerogatives. The college, on the other hand, has responsibility for the teacher-education program. Accreditation places responsibility on the college, not the public school system, for such things as the selection of student-teachers and the marking of student-teachers. I do not think that this should be a delegated responsibility for the level at which it marks its students.

Now on all of these things, of course, consultation is a very important dimension in communication, and this emphasizes all the business of conferences, meetings, and committees in which people get together to participate in arriving at these decisions, making recommendations to each other and ironing out rough spots. I would strongly advocate that administrators, supervisory personnel, and classroom teachers from both college and public schools be involved. You would thus have people from the college level who are responsible for administration, people who are in supervisory positions, and people who teach college courses in methods and what-have-you. There should be no need for protection against exploitation in either direction, and it can be avoided if there is a good effort at mutual understanding and respect for each other's recommendations through frequent committee meetings.

I was interested in your comments concerning the general methods course and I agree very, very strongly. I think that this is the course which, above all others, brings down the wrath of everyone upon teacher education. The general methods course is one which ought to be abolished. This fits into the middle of a long chain and this chain strings on and on and on. My friends in liberal arts colleges, however, point up a problem they often have: If educational psychology is taught in the psychology department, and the content methods course, the special methods course, is taught in the academic department, they say the only place they have a chance to influence the student before student teaching is in the general methods course. I'll personally accept the validity of that concern and then urge these people to try to solve the problem.

We have referred several times in this conference to a matter which I think has not been well spelled out; we've come up to it and then we've slid away from it. It's been inferred and it's been actually identified, but let me stress it. This matter is the two levels in certification. You had it in the diagram you drew on the board yesterday, Mr. Bush, in which there is an initial level of certification and then later, after further experiences and work and endorsement, there is final full certification. Here is certainly an area in which colleges and the public school systems need to work very closely together. Many colleges feel that, well, now they're off our hands and the public school systems can have them from here. I recall the annual speech by a superintendent, in a city where the college in which I worked was located, who always said at his opening meeting for new faculty members: "The first thing I want you to do is to forget everything they taught you in that college over there and let us show you how to teach in the classroom." But I think we need to come together with carefully planned programs of mutual responsibility for the further education of beginning teachers. The same is true for older teachers' continuing education. The things you're doing in this area, Mr. Barnes, are very, very exciting. I was interested, too, in how you came back to the need for skills. There we were again with Mr. Bush's emphasis on skills.

Another area we might touch on very briefly is that of the pre-student-teaching experience. I am not one who thinks too highly of observational visits by large numbers of students. I think we can do this better by the new techniques and the new technology. But I'm thinking of such things as pre-student-teaching classroom experiences in which the student has a chance to go into a classroom, if only for a short period of time, to work with an experienced teacher. Or, interestingly enough, why not even with a student-teacher? Let's say we have a senior student-teacher who has been at work for a few weeks and then takes on a junior for even just a few days. The senior student-teacher then finds it necessary to verbalize, to express, to guide, and to show seniority; all these things bring out the best in individuals, and the junior returning to his education classroom would have a much better understanding of what is needed and expected when he will be a student-teacher some months hence.

Let me close by saying that invitational conferences, large and small, to which supervising teachers from the public schools might come, perhaps, when they can leave their classes in the hands of an experienced student-teacher toward the latter part of the term, can be well utilized. Joint appointments further the exchange job, three weeks in each direction. I thought this was a very interesting thing here at Stanford, Mr. Bush. The sabbatical, the supervisor on leave, or the public school teacher on leave who takes a term as a supervising teacher in the student-teaching program—all of these things offer many opportunities for public school cooperation with colleges and college cooperation with the schools. But the big need is communication, not meetings and conferences *ad infinitum*, but communication among key people (not forgetting the classroom teacher)! This is our big need in teacher education, along with the recognition of mutual responsibility of the college and the public school you brought out so very well in your remarks.

COGAN: I think it might be profitable to spend some time on the concept Mr. Mork developed when he spoke about the two institutions and the problem of bringing them together. If I recall correctly, he spoke about the need of the university not to encroach upon, not to usurp the responsibilities of the public schools, and I think vice versa also. I'd like for a moment to entertain an idea diametrically opposed to this. A popular view is that the school's responsibility, *the* responsibility, is instruction. And I think it's at this point that I should like to ask a question. I don't really believe this popular view. I think that the school has told itself it has *a* responsibility but that truly it has *two* responsibilities. One is for instruction and the other is for the improvement of instruction. If you will accept this additional assumption, then we've got to abandon the concept of two sovereign nations—the school and the university—joined by some sort of treaty. You know, they get along nicely and they exchange ambassadors and the like. I think that what we really have to look at is the possibility of some concept of overlapping sovereignty so that, for example, the people at the university may be able to join in policy making of certain kinds. Perhaps the schools should be making policy which would occasionally risk the instruction of pupils for research purposes or for purposes of inducting teachers. I don't really want to elaborate this any further. I think also that both institutions ought to risk some money in this joint operation. In any event, the concept of partially overlapping sovereignty may be useful in the kinds of problems we're dealing with.

DAVIES: The new USOE-financed regional laboratories offer an interesting opportunity for testing out the overlapping sovereignty idea to see if it works.

BOYAN: I'd like to suggest a third possibility, that the schools unabashedly would, with knowledge and malice aforethought, make every effort to exploit the university, but at least know why they want to and how to go about doing it. I have no concern about my university colleagues protecting themselves in any kind of relationship with the school system in its attempts to exploit, and I'm sure most of you have good colleagues who can well protect themselves in this kind of arrangement. I think it goes back to the notion—and this may be the heart of the whole matter—that implicitly and for the most part explicitly, school systems operate on the basic assumption, even though they protest otherwise, that the beginning teacher is a finished product. I will take the other position, mostly because our preparation programs are not long enough and perhaps never should be because of the number of people who don't stay in teaching anyway. Our preparation programs are not long enough to warrant the assumption that the individual is a finished product. And especially against the notion of two levels of certification, I would go further and say that until specific criteria have been established and made public, and until a person has completed his preparation program at a university and worked in the school system—until he has reached criterion level—he should not be permitted to practice with full responsibility in the classroom. The notion that the beginning teacher should be permitted to teach on his own basically with full responsibility for whole classes of boys and girls just does not make good public sense. In a way it's a prostitution of the whole operation. We bring people in and we admit they are not fully prepared because, first of all, they are not even on tenure yet; secondly, we insist on the notion of in-service training. In spite of these two items, we then throw young teachers into the classroom situation with full responsibility, with relatively little systematic supervision, if any, and then we ask ourselves about this question of school-university relations.

Now suppose you took the other proposition. Suppose every school system adopted the postulate that it would not let a beginning teacher assume the responsibility of full-time practice until senior members of the faculty of those school systems, who perhaps have more competence to make the judgments than our existing supervisors and administrators, welcome the probationer into post-probationary status. At that point allow him full responsibility, or make him accountable to his colleagues for full-time responsibility. Under these conditions the school system could very well take the position that everybody who begins practice in this school system must go through a continuation of training in which there is clear willingness to accept the position and to make it public that there is an attempt to shape behavior. This gets us away from the group process approach of the Association for Supervision and Curriculum Development and says, specifically, that school system supervisors of the beginning teachers have the responsibility to shape behavior toward certain criteria. Then they call on a relationship with the university to do two kinds of things: 1) Make those criteria explicit and public, and 2) then ask the university to help train the supervisors who in turn are going to help shape the behavior of the beginning teachers.

SCHUELER: I'm glad to be able to publicly acknowledge that on this point we agree. I think many of us have been worried about this particular problem and have been pushing this idea of lengthening the induction period of teachers for full-time regular service. Mr. Bush has been talking about this for years. Of course what we have to recognize here is that if we place greater responsibility on the service aspect in the schools two things have to happen: 1) There has to be developed the kind of very close working relationship that was mentioned this morning between the school and the university, and 2) the roles of the various people in the schools have not only to be defined but people have to be trained to assume these roles. The way we have developed, i.e., with a tradition of separateness, it may very well be true that if we put this responsibility prematurely on the school and our colleagues without a thorough consideration of what it means and what kind of training the supervisory people need in order to judge beginning teachers, then the whole thing may fall flat. But I do think there are movements afoot, as mentioned today, in very many places, where this close cooperation and this kind of defining of roles is proceeding.

Just to give you an example that is very much akin to what is happening in Portland (this is probably not known well outside of New York City), every single one of the teacher-training institutions in the metropolitan area of New York, both public and private, is involved intimately in a movement that the New York City school system calls the "Campus School Movement." There are over 100 schools directly affiliated with individual teacher-training universities. The intent was first to bring them together to create campus schools in the community. Now, of course, in the first go-around the results and the conceptions on both the side of the schools and the universities are quite varied, so some of them are rather nominal performers, while some of them have become quite intimate, to the extent that several of our institutions are even going to be affiliated. And, significantly enough, the design of these buildings is for two purposes which we hope are complementary: 1) We hope to enhance the training processes, and 2) to enhance the improvement process. Therefore we're all looking for buildings of infinite flexibility so they can be used for all kinds of purposes. But I think it must be said here that this is the ideal. I think we all will agree it has to happen. It's not enough. There have developed and there will continue to develop many tensions in this relationship. It is in the nature of the university professor to feel that he has a broader view, that he is closer to the cutting edge (even though sometimes he may not be) of curriculum development and methodology. And it is in the nature of the school person to feel that, by golly, he is in the "real" role and he knows what he is doing. And yet they cannot operate one without the other. This partnership is a very difficult one, I think; there's no partnership which is more difficult or is subject to more tensions, but we simply have to make it work.

There is one alternative, Mr. Barnes, to your clinical professorship. I think it has been used in many places and has certain advantages. That is to withhold a proportion of staff positions, particularly those that have to do with the area of methodology, etc., and student-teaching supervision, for school personnel on what we in New York call the "Lend-Lease Program." Teachers in the schools who are known to be master teachers or supervisors are brought to the colleges for one year (sometimes for two) with identical salaries and the same pensions; the whole thing is just shifted right over. We assume their entire salary, even though in some cases the salary of the teacher on maximum is considerably above that of an associate professor at the college; but we don't have to worry about that since we just take them over for a year. They work with our students and with the staff and then go back to the school system afterwards. There's one frustrating part of this arrangement: There's also the other side of the coin; we have an arrangement that any member of a college staff may engage in reverse lend-lease and may be taken over by the school system for a year in return for a teacher who comes to the college. Well, we have literally hundreds of requests from public school personnel to come to the college each year. So far (and we have struggled over this) in the last five years we have had one college person who has spent a year in a school system—and the New York City school system isn't quite as bad as sometimes shown. Let's face it—the school teachers just have to work harder.

BROUDY: I would be false to my role if I didn't manage to make an observation on this paper, but in order not to be misunderstood, or rather not to be understood too well, I must say something by way of preface. I want to declare my un-limited admiration and applause for the kinds of things Super-intendent Barnes describes, the heroic attempts to get some kind of relationship between the universities and the school systems. I would only wish that we could put as much ingenuity into turning out a good product in the first place as we do in patching up the baling-wire product we do turn out. May I quickly give a little evidence? Mr. Barnes interviewed people and he has read papers, as we all have, about the criticism of teacher training. Because they are monotonously alike, I think we can generalize these criticisms. They sound like this: The people you turn out from the colleges of education just don't have the high-grade intellect and professional competence to do all the things that parents and enlightened people want them to do. Second, colleges of education are reluctant to in-novate in the teacher-training program. Everybody knows that we (the critics) are eager to innovate, but the teacher-training professors are not. Third, every investigation discloses that de-spite all the heroic remedial measures, most of the teachers are in a deplorable state. In other words, these are, at most, *ad hoc* measures, and, unfortunately, the remediated teachers don't stay in the schoolroom long; we have to do it all over again.

We have to have *ad hoc* remedies for these problems, be-cause we have made it pretty certain that we're going to need them. By reducing the teacher-training curriculum to the very minimum we have created a situation where if anything is going to be done for the professional side of the training it will have to be done by in-service methods. We turn out mechanics and then we make automotive engineers out of them by in-service training. Perhaps the real innovation would be to acknowledge once and for all that the baling-wire and glue notion of educating teachers isn't adequate for what we need. Maybe the innovation is really to invest time in a really professional program for the training of teachers. Maybe the graduates of such a program would stay longer. Maybe we wouldn't have to give them shots in the head every summer. Physicians also take in-service training, but they don't make their in-service training the heart of the program and they do not regard pre-service training as a deplorable prelude which somehow can't be avoided. We are reaching a state of affairs where the remedial measures themselves indicate that the fundamental structure of the abbreviated training program is just not strong enough even to carry the remedial measures. With that cheerful note I leave you, because I have to catch a plane.

BUSH: The note that has just been sounded is a good one. We cannot, however, take *ad hoc* arrangements with the teacher-training institutions and put them together with *ad hoc* remedial arrangements in the schools and hope that with cooperation we'll get something constructive out of it. We are making some progress. Until recently we did not even talk about the matter. Mr. Barnes' speech suggests that we are beginning to talk properly about it now. But the next step will be an extremely long and difficult one to take.

There is a critical time in the training of teachers which I have referred to as *the formative years*, the time when young people leave training and move out into practice. We must look at this not as two things, pre-service and in-service, but as the most crucial time in the preparation of teachers. We still cling, it seems to me, to the archaic idea that the colleges and universities produce teachers and the schools consume them. At times I am optimistic, although when I see some of the *ad hoc* arrangements we make I find little reason for optimism. I want to refer back to Mr. Schueler's comments of yesterday. If, as we amass resources for the underprivileged schools and saturate them with help, we could at the same time saturate resources during the formative years, we might make double progress. As I indicated yesterday, if we could prepare teachers to teach

160

in the kind of schools Mr. Schueler was talking about, such teachers could probably teach anywhere. With sufficient resources properly to prepare teachers for underprivileged schools, we would not have to rely on *ad hoc* arrangements.

BOYAN: Mr. Davies, it seems to me that this kind of alternative would make something a lot more powerful for the profession to support than the emergency Teacher Corps idea. Take the resources that were tentatively earmarked, or hopefully earmarked, for the Teacher Corps and put them into a program which involves specifically designed continuity rather than the notion of a pre- or in-service arrangement.

DAVIES: First, Mr. Boyan, two of the new research and development centers (the one here at Stanford and one at the University of Texas) have teacher education as their focus. Unless both of these centers generate the kinds of concepts you're talking about and produce new wisdom on these problems, we will not be using ten million dollars as constructively as we want. If we simply produce better technology so we can do a better job with micro-teaching, for example, this would be useful, but it would not be a good way to spend that much money. The ten million dollars should lead us to the solution of fundamental problems.

BARNES: I think that in the development of closer school and university relationships there are probably more barriers residing in the public school systems than there are in the universities. It's common for schoolmen, as has been indicated here today, to employ a new teacher and then to discover that the new teacher has difficulties and immediately blame the preparing institution. This is perhaps more characteristic of small school systems. Obviously, a newly employed teacher cannot be expected to have developed very far in handling the problems of his profession. Some teachers who on their first jobs experience considerable difficulty turn out to be the best teachers. School systems must put money into staff development. It takes money for in-service education, for travel, for curriculum development; and unless the school system sees this as important and finances it, it's not going to get anywhere with in-service education.

LAWRENCE: I understand that letting anybody talk on this side of that line [indicating line between discussants and audience] destroys the position, but I'm a long-time Phi Delta Kappan and I want to contribute. I want to ask you a question: To what extent does the conception of teacher education you've been talking about include the preparation of para-professionals, sub-professionals, or whatever you want to call the group that's going to receive a lot of support out of the new Office of Economic Opportunity programs? Are they a part of this? Does teacher education, as you're talking about it, include these people or are they another problem?

BOYAN: I think Mr. Lawrence's question prompts one kind of reaction that might be useful in general as we think about preparation of people for various kinds of jobs. That which can best be done in the university should be done in the university; that which can best be done in the school should be done in the school. My hunch is that the preparation of para-professionals can best be done in the school; therefore I would say, let us do it in the school and not bother the universities with the task.

LAWRENCE: I have a question for either Mr. Bellack or Mr. Bush. Considering the time and energy and ability it takes to acquire skill and judgment in influencing people's behavior, I wonder what your reaction is to the clinical-professor concept Conant has expounded on.

BUSH: Let me see if I understand the question. It is a very complicated matter to prepare people to try to influence behavior. Is your question, "Can you really expect to take a person from the classroom and make a clinical professor of him so he can do this job?"

LAWRENCE: That's precisely it.

BUSH: My answer is unequivocally yes. One of the reasons we have not done better is that we have not drawn upon the creative, imaginative, insightful experience of the best practitioners in the schools. If we would draw upon them more and put them into training positions we would have much better training. If we could couple this experience with the material which is beginning to flow out of the research centers being established we could create a powerful kind of position. I don't think these people in between—the clinical professors—can do it all. So this is a plea for cooperation. The idea of the clinical professor has been drawn out of context, distorted, and used in a variety of ways. I still think it is a viable idea to use the very best teachers in the schools as cooperative partners in the teacher-training process. This is one way to bring about a marriage of research and practice. Many of our problems in research and development and in understanding the processes of teaching and teacher education arise from a lack of relationship between the two. We have not used, in research about teaching, those who are working in it. One objective is to train teachers who themselves will not only teaach but who will also thoughtfully study the process itself, thereby contributing to research on teaching.

ADJOURNMENT

Chapter VI

Breakthrough in Teacher Education?

By James C. Stone
Professor of Education and Director of Teacher Education
University of California, Berkeley

> We are entering upon an era which will test to the
> utmost the capacity of our democracy to cope with the
> gravest problems of modern times. . . . We are entering
> upon this difficult and dangerous period with what I be-
> lieve we must call a growing deficit in the quantity and
> quality of American education. We have to make a *break-*
> *through* to radically higher and broader conception of
> what is needed and what can be done. Our educational
> effort today . . . is still in approximately the same position
> as was the military effort of this country before Pearl
> Harbor.
>
> *Walter Lippmann* (1954)

With this as a theme, the Ford Foundation began to give
large amounts of money for what it thought might be accomplished by way of a breakthrough in education. In particular,
the Foundation provided some seventy million dollars to mount
a sustained effort to make a breakthrough in the education of
teachers. Now, ten to fifteen years later, what, in fact, has been
accomplished?

My particular assignment, for the past two years, was to
take a hard look at the result of this investment of venture
capital and attempt to determine whether some sort of breakthrough in the education of teachers actually had occurred. Specifically, my assignment was to study the programs which had
been supported in the previous five years,[1] to evaluate the

---

[1] James C. Stone, "Twenty-nine Million *for What?*" *CTA Journal*,
October, 1964.

success of these efforts, to find out what had been learned and what use was being made of what had been learned—in a word, to find out what has been the impact of the use of this venture capital.

The investigation took a year and a half, much of it spent visiting the colleges and universities and their cooperating school systems. In all, forty-two colleges and universities operating forty-three of these "breakthrough" programs were examined. Different kinds of institutions are represented among the forty-two—small private liberal arts colleges, large private universities, large and small state universities—they varied from those which were undergraduate institutions to those with extensive offerings on the doctoral level. Four of the institutions prepared only elementary school teachers, twenty-three secondary only, and fourteen both elementary and secondary. The list of institutions and curriculum types is given in Table I.

The chief means of data gathering were three: 1) analysis of the reports, records, and evaluative information in the files of the Ford Foundation in New York; 2) the use of several questionnaires which were specifically designed to elicit information from the institutions and their cooperating schools regarding the impact of their experimental efforts; and 3) a three- or four-day visit on each of these campuses in order to interview students in the programs as well as students who had graduated from the programs, teachers and administrators in the field, and academic and education staffs in the institutions—both those who were involved in the new programs and those who had nothing to do with them.

At the conclusion of the visits, another six months were spent in preparing a monograph for publication by the Foundation. The monograph begins with six chapters which relate in a case-study form what happened in six different institutions with six different programs as follows: "Comrades of the Quest," a descriptive analysis of the program at Reed College; "Ekcolu Ame Elua," which describes and analyzes the program at the University of Hawaii, in cooperation with the Hawaiian State Department of Education; "Catalyst at Work," a title chosen for what occurred at Webster College; "Up by Their Bootstraps" (The University of North Carolina at Chapel Hill);

166

"Experiment on the Farm" (Stanford University); and finally, Anatomy of a Failure" (Miami University).

Following these six case studies are a chapter on the six undergraduate programs, a chapter on the eleven five- and fifth-year programs, and an extensive chapter on the twenty-five MAT-type programs.

The report of the investigation concludes with a section titled "Overall Impact." This paper draws heavily from that chapter and summarizes the major accomplishments of the breakthrough effort as well as its major deficiencies, offering some thoughts regarding possible new directions for teacher education which appear to have been identified and substantiated.

MAJOR ACCOMPLISHMENTS

High Quality Teachers

While admittedly open to accusations of bias and subjectivity, from individual and group interviews with interns and externs, from comments by academic and education faculty, from opinions openly expressed by school supervising teachers, principals, and central office personnel, there is an overwhelming consensus that *a* major, perhaps *the* major, asset of the experimental curricula is the quality of the women and men attracted to and graduating from the program. As people, as scholars, and as teachers, they are top-drawer. As a group, they are impressive on any one of a number of criteria—personality, appearance, commitment to teaching, and leadership qualities. (It would be surprising, in fact, if they were not outstanding individuals, since they are specially recruited and carefully selected prior to admission to the program and are usually painstakingly tended during its year of operation. Both they and the program are regarded as "special" and they tend to think of themselves and each other as "special.")

Two-thirds of the trainees were women, but the men were of equally high caliber. Supported by a unanimity of subjective opinions, the conclusion seems inescapable that exceptionally well qualified men and women are entering teaching today through the breakthrough programs. In a number of institutions,

Table I

Types of Programs and Teaching Levels of Each, by Institution

Institution	Types of Programs			Teaching Levels		
	Under-grad.	Five & Fifth Year	MAT	Elem. Only	Sec. Only	Both Elem. & Sec.
Barnard	X				X	
Brown			X		X	
Buffalo		X			X	
California (at L. A.)		X				X
*Carnegie Tech			X		X	
Chicago			X		X	
Central Michigan		X				X
Claremont		X				X
Converse			X		X	
**Cornell		X			X	
Duke			X		X	
Emory			X			X
Fairleigh Dickinson			X		X	
George Peabody			X			X
George Washington		X		X		
Hawaii		X				X
Harvard			X		X	
Indiana			X			X
Johns Hopkins			X		X	
Kansas State			X		X	
Maine			X			X
Marshall	X					X
Miami (of Ohio)			X			X
Michigan State	X			X		
Middlebury	X					X
Missouri (at K. C.)	X					X
New York University		X		X		
North Carolina			X		X	
Northwestern			X		X	
Notre Dame			X		X	
Oberlin			X		X	
Pittsburgh			X			X
Reed			X		X	
Rochester		X			X	
Stanford			X		X	
Southern California			X		X	
Syracuse		X			X	
Vanderbilt			X		X	
Wayne State			X			X
***Webster	X			X		
Wisconsin		X				X
Yale			X		X	
Total - 42	6	11	25	4	23	15

* Carnegie Tech also offered a four-year undergraduate and a fifth-year program.
** Cornell has two grants, one for junior high school and one for high school, thus accounting for the 43 programs in the 42 colleges and universities.
*** Webster also offered an MAT for in-service teachers, completed in five summers.

data on the qualifications of the students are being accumulated. In a few instances, comparative studies between conventional and Ford-grant program students are under way. Both kinds of data, though largely as yet unpublished and incomplete, support the quality generalization about Ford-grant graduates.

Tapping a New Source of Teacher Supply

A purpose of Ford-grant programs was to tap new sources of teacher supply, particularly those not normally attracted to teaching via conventional curricula. Such people are housewives now seeking careers, returning military personnel, older, more mature men seeking new careers, and liberal arts graduates of all kinds and ages. The number completing Ford-grant programs reveals the extent to which this purpose has been accomplished.

In the three-year period 1961-62 through 1963-64, 4,114 students completed Ford-grant programs. This is an average output of 1,371 per year. All but 830 of the 4,114 were prepared for secondary teaching. The number completing the programs in any single year ranged from seven at Converse College to 335 at Harvard.

As shown in Table II, in those institutions which also offered a parallel conventional program of teacher education, 24,703 students completed this type of curriculum. This was an average output of 8,234 per year. Again, the majority (59 percent) were prepared for secondary school teaching.

While the "completion" figures for Ford-grant programs are modest in comparison with those of the longer-established conventional programs, the Ford-grant increase—a doubling in the three-year period—is impressive.

Six of the Ford-grant programs were completed by a sizeable number of students; for example, 869 at Harvard, 319 at Wisconsin, 213 at Brown, 209 at Pittsburgh, and 201 at Stanford. These six institutions accounted for 44 percent of the total number completing Ford-grant programs in the three-year period. Enrollment trends in Ford-grant and conventional programs, as shown by numbers completing teacher education curricula, are shown in Table II.

Table II

Number Completing Ford-grant and Conventional Programs, 1961-62 through 1963-64

Year	Number Who Completed Ford-grant Program as			Number Who Completed Conventional Program as		
	Elementary School Teachers	Secondary School Teachers	Total	Elementary School Teachers	Secondary School Teachers	Total
1961-62	196	819	1,015	3,338	4,791	8,129
1962-63	226	946	1,172	3,297	4,691	7,988
1963-64	408	1,519	1,927	3,561	5,025	8,586
Totals	830	3,284	4,114*	10,196	14,507	24,703

*Because several Ford-grant programs had students who had not yet completed the program, figures from these programs were not included. The programs omitted for this reason were: Carnegie Tech, Indiana, Webster, Marshall, Hawaii, and UCLA.

While some students in the Ford-grant program may have been recruited at the expense of the institutions' regular programs, this number is likely small since the number of students completing conventional curricula also increased during the period. Thus it would appear that the 4,114 who finished Ford-grant curricula largely represent additions to the nation's pool of qualified first-year teachers. The doubling of enrollment in the three-year program would seem to indicate the increasing drawing power of these experimental projects, especially for secondary school teaching.

Quality programs appeal to and attract quality candidates. In interview after interview, students in Ford-grant programs said they would not have entered teaching if the only route available had been the conventional one.

Professional Staying Power

It has long been known that many students completing teacher education curricula do not immediately enter teaching and, at least for the moment, are considered lost to the profession. For example, one state-wide study reported:

> Placement officers in the teacher education institutions were requested to report on follow-up studies of their 1957 credential candidates. The reports of their studies showed that 75.12 percent of the candidates for secondary teaching credentials and 82.06 percent of the candidates for elementary teaching credentials who had completed work for teaching credentials in June had accepted positions in the public schools of California by September 30, 1957. Of the total number of persons who completed credential requirements, 79.1 percent had entered teaching by September 30, 1957. . . . Reports in 1956 showed that 56.96 percent of the successful credential candidates had accepted teaching positions by September 30, 1956. In 1955, the percent was 44.98.[2]

A later report stated: "Follow-up studies of previous years indicated that any June list of potential teachers would be reduced by approximately 27 percent by September."[3]

Because the nation's prime source of new teachers is among those students who complete programs of teacher education each year, data on the professional "staying power" of these new-type programs was secured. The Ford-grant institutions were asked to indicate what course of action each student undertook upon completion of Ford and conventional curricula during the period under review.

In 1961-62 and 1962-63, 2,187 teachers were reported to have successfully completed Ford-grant programs. All but twenty-two were secondary school candidates. The institutions reported that 1,714 or 78 percent of these 2,187 were engaged in teaching following graduation, another 137 were involved in educational work of some other kind, and 336 forsook educational work for a different activity. Breakdowns of the figures follow.

Teaching: 1,530 in public schools, 105 in private schools,

---

[2] "Teachers for California's Schools, 1958-1970," *Bulletin of the California State Department of Education*, Vol. XXVII, No. 1, February, 1959, p. 15.

[3] James C. Stone, *California's Commitment to Public Education*. New York: Thomas Y. Crowell Co., 1961, p. 30.

42 in schools in foreign countries, and 37 in colleges or universities.

Other Educational Endeavor: 115 continued as students in a college or university, 12 became librarians, and 10 became curriculum consultants, supervisors, or principals.

Other Activity: 23 joined the Peace Corps, 39 became housewives, 27 entered military service, 41 were employed by business or industry, and 206 were listed as "not known" at the time the information was requested.

In the same two-year period, 16,117 completed the conventional teacher education programs in these institutions.[4] These graduates (6,635 prepared for elementary teaching, 9,482 for secondary) were reported engaged in these activities following graduation: 7,898 or 49 percent were teaching, 881 were in some other educational work, and 7,338 or 46 percent forsook teaching for some other activity. Breakdowns follow:

Teaching: 7,654 in public schools, 186 in private schools, 18 in schools in foreign countries, and 40 taught in colleges or universities.

Other Educational Endeavor: 825 continued as college or university students, 88 became librarians, 28 became curriculum consultants, supervisors, or principals.

Other Activity: 8 joined the Peace Corps, 76 became housewives, 76 were employed by business or industry, 49 entered military service, and 7,129 were listed as "not known" at the time the information was requested.

A comparison in the staying power of the Ford and conventional programs is striking, with 85 percent of Ford "graduates" in education as compared with only 54 percent of conventional graduates. It must be noted, however, that poor follow-up of graduates in the conventional programs left 44 percent unaccounted for. Some of these may have taken teaching positions. The degree to which the Ford programs have been able to keep track of their graduates is significant.

Follow-up studies of other experimental programs than those financed by Ford indicate that the staying power of the

[4]Excludes several such as Claremont, Maine, Yale, and Harvard in which the Ford-grant type program is the only program offered.

Ford-grant programs compares favorably. For example, a six-year follow-up study of the Graduate Internship Program in Teacher Education at the University of California (Berkeley), published in 1965, reported:

> Taken as a group, the "staying power" of interns in the profession is impressive. After six years, nearly half of the 1956 group still are teaching (Table III). Three-fourths of the 1957 and 1958 groups still are teaching after five and four years respectively. Approximately four-fifths of the 1959 group are teaching after three years, and nine-tenths of the 1960 group after two years. One hundred percent of the 1961 group completed one year of teaching.[5]

An unpublished follow-up study at Harvard University reported:

> Of all MAT-earners in the first decade after World War II, about 60 percent of the women and 82 percent of the men are still confirmed teachers. Most important, 80 percent of those still teaching are in public schools and public colleges.[6]

From the Harvard data and similar unpublished reports available at a number of the institutions visited, it seems safe to conclude that the professional staying power of the graduates of Ford-sponsored programs (and similar non-Ford-sponsored programs) is impressive. Nothing could be more important in solving the undersupply-overdemand problem in teaching than recruiting and preparing candidates who stay at the important job of teaching. That the "Ford graduates" also represent a plus on the quality scale adds to the importance of their finding satisfactions in the classroom. In short, the Ford Foundation supported programs give evidence of having attracted quality candidates, given them a unique preparation, and delivered a higher percentage of them into teaching—persons who stayed longer in teaching and taught effectively. These are measures of their productivity.

---

[5] James C. Stone and Clark N. Robinson, *The Graduate Internship Program in Teacher Education: The First Six Years*. University of California Publications in Education, Vol. 15. Berkeley and Los Angeles: University of California Press, 1965, p. 79.

[6] Study referred to in "The Harvard Touch," *Time*, Vol. 81, No. 6, February 8, 1963, p. 50.

Table III

Percent of Interns Who Remained in Teaching

Duration of Employment

Intern Group	Internship Year	First Post-Internship Year	Second Post-Internship Year	Third Post-Internship Year	Fourth Post-Internship Year	Fifth Post-Internship Year
1956	100	94	77	59	42	47
1957	100	93	74	79	74	—
1958	100	87	81	73	—	—
1959	100	89	79	—	—	—
1960	100	91	—	—	—	—
1961	100	—	—	—	—	—

174

Another subjective conclusion, but one which again is supported by a consensus of institutional and school personnel, as well as by unsolicited endorsements and commendations by interns and externs, is that the directors and their immediate staff were innovators in their respective institutions. Often the directors were referred to as "the excitement men" on the campus, and these "excitment men" seemed to attach similar types as staff associates. Some of the directors were former professors of English, history, biology, or mathematics, some were professors of education, others were drawn directly from administrative positions in the schools. But from whatever source, they had leadership qualities *par excellence*. In the final analysis, it would appear that the Foundation, having met and assessed these men, placed its grant as a bet on leadership.

With this leadership ability, one could easily identify concomitant characteristics which participants in the new programs possessed—high morale among students and staff; close and warm personal relations between student and student, staff and staff, and staff and students; *esprit de corps*, partly because they all knew they were different, were being observed and were in fact involved in an experiment, but also because they shared common experiences and came to know, respect, and admire one another, and to be proud of their identity with the new program. Perhaps the best evidence on this latter point is that the graduates sell their "friends and relations" on the program, and these become a corps of the next year's group of trainees.

Academic Support

It has become a cliché in teacher education today to talk about "the responsibility of the total institution," the "all-institutional approach," or "cooperation between education and academic faculties." So it is not unexpected to be able to conclude that in forty-one of the forty-two institutions there was a high degree of such good working relationships. These relationships appeared to be equally vital regardless of the institutional pattern of organization for teacher education.

Whether it was a school or college of education within a university, a department of education in a liberal arts college, or no identifiable education unit as at Yale, Barnard, and Webster, all forms of organization seemed to make for cooperative relationships because, within these new curricula and within the minds of those who were involved in designing and operating them, there was a new spirit of working together toward a common goal.

But what was more surprising than a finding of cooperation and high spirit was the degree of support for, interest in, and commitment to the experimental programs on the part of academic professors, particularly those in English, the social sciences, the life sciences, foreign languages, and, to a somewhat lesser extent, mathematics. The reason for this may be related in part to the fact that it is students with these majors who make up the bulk of those in the experimental programs. But for whatever reason, their support was substantial. Often it was in sharp contrast to the lack of support for these same breakthrough curricula from the regular staffs in schools and colleges. The reason here is not hard to find: Some doubtless felt threatened, some were repelled by the extensive publicity and attention given to the smallest feature or event in the new program, many by temperament and experience were wedded to the conventional curriculum and believed in its importance and its contribution to the education of the American teacher.

Subject-Matter Emphasis

The other side of the coin marked "support by academic departments" is a renaissance in the place of academic subject matter in the programs of teachers prepared through the experimental curricula. To some degree this came about through the use of new funds to immediately infuse into traditional majors the newest in science, mathematics, foreign languages, and other fields less dramatically changed by the knowledge explosion. To a large measure it came about through the extension of the preparation period through a master's degree. In MAT-type as well as five- and fifth-year programs, the candidate was able to build on an already strong undergraduate academic major, which was one important basis of admission to the new programs. The number of units in a teaching field taken in the post-graduate period varied from eight to twenty-four. At two institutions, the University of Southern California and the University of Chicago, the candidate was expected to complete the equivalent of a master's degree in a subject field in addition to his education work in order to qualify for the MAT degree. In all programs, including the six undergraduate curricula, additional time for subject matter concentration was made available through a reduction of requirements in professional education to "an irreducible minimum." A rather typical comment of schoolmen was that "these students really know their subjects and have confidence that they can teach them."

Few today would doubt the value of such teachers for America's secondary *and* elementary classrooms. Clearly, the new curricula have here demonstrated their contribution and the appropriateness of a master's degree as a feasible goal in the pre-service education of specially qualified teachers. Regardless of title (Master of Arts, Master of Education, Master of Arts in Education, Master of Science) the degrees in the twenty-five MAT-type programs represent a neat blend of academic and professional studies.

At a number of institutions, important gains have been made through the use of the MAT degree for teachers in service. The in-service appeal of the MAT was particularly noticeable at Brown, Maine, Northwestern, and Reed.

The Teaching Internship

At the heart of many of these programs has been a teaching internship, a laboratory experience which differs markedly from student teaching in intensity and extensity. Its major difference is that it is a responsible, paid teaching assignment in which the intern is legally accountable for the instruction. It differs, too, in that while student teaching is usually the *culminating* experience in the professional sequence, an internship is the *central* aspect of the professional sequence, usually with courses in education, called seminars, revolving around the teaching act. In breakthrough programs in which students were most enthusiastic about their experiences, the internship program was pre-

177

ceded by a summer of education work and student teaching, and concurrent seminars were continued during and after the teaching internship experience. Thus in these programs clinical practice became the core of the professional work in education. The student was involved in both a stream of experience and a parallel stream of theory. With the help of his instructors, each stream contributed to his development as a competent practitioner.

While not all programs actually operated this way, many attempted to. The difficulty is that integration of the theory-practice component is easy to talk and write about but it is very difficult to achieve. It requires more time for planning and evaluation than conventional plans of operation and it takes a staff suited by temperament to work with each other and by experience and conviction to teach, supervise, and guide students.

School-College Alliance

Related to the new conception of professional education is the bringing of the public schools into a more vital role in the professional aspects of teacher preparation. School principals and supervisors often were not only involved in the selection, assignment, and evaluation of interns, but many served as "clinical professors" for the concurrent seminars. Some participated as demonstration teachers in the specially organized summer schools for elementary or secondary school children which often became the center of the interns' initial summer of pre-internship preparation. In addition, a number of the schools themselves were experimenting with new teaching innovations and arrangements for instruction and thus interns were given opportunities to experience the new instructional media at first hand.

Public school personnel so involved often spoke of the program as "our program." Thus there has occurred a breakdown of the traditional dichotomy of pre-service and in-service education: the colleges' obligation versus the public schools' responsibility. Teacher growth is a continuing process and each group is now involved in both parts. The prospective teacher and her pupils are the chief ones to gain from this new alliance of resources.

Variation in Approaches

One of the most frequently heard criticisms of the Ford Foundation's grants in teacher education, beginning with its first effort in 1951, was that it had a prescription for curing the ills of American education and the money to demonstrate the effectiveness of its remedy. Among institutions not participating in these experiments, it was (and is) popular to say that they just didn't care to "buy" the particular brand of patent medicine the Foundation was selling.

Anyone who has visited these forty-two institutions, or who examines the data from this study, cannot help being impressed by the variety of measures used by institutions and program directors to accomplish the same objectives. The general flexibility inherent in the experimental approaches stands out, as do the many ways that have been devised to solve the same problems. Compare, for example, the use of real clinical experiences in the pre-internship summer program at the University of California at Berkeley with the simulated laboratory method used at Stanford University. Two more different methods hardly could be found. Both come from the "no holds barred" freedom to be experimental provided by venture capital.

Institutional Take-over

With the lone exception of Miami, all of the experimental curricula have been or are in the process of being taken over by the institutions, in whole or in part. At eleven—Barnard, Brown, Claremont, Harvard, Maine, Middlebury, Missouri, Notre Dame, Reed, Stanford, and Yale—the new curriculum has become the standard curriculum and the former conventional pattern of teacher education has been abandoned. At several others, major modifications are occurring in their standard curriculum. In most cases, both "old" and "new" programs are being continued as parallel avenues into teaching. The decisions in these instances were made on the belief that a variety of people are atracted to teaching and that multiple paths are required since no one plan

179

serves the needs of all. As one university president put it, "There is no singular royal road to higher education, nor is there one for teacher education."

Related to the confidence of institutions in the breakthrough programs as witnessed by their willingness to provide budget for the new and additional curricula is the fact that it is likely none of these experiments would have been undertaken without Foundation support. The innovations were simply too radical and risky for institutions to finance. Venture capital, therefore, accepted the risk in supporting these new approaches. If all had failed, this still would have been an appropriate activity for the Foundation to have engaged in. It is especially in the area of great risk that venture capital plays the most important and unique role. In fact, its chief obligation is to play the hunches no one else can afford to bet on.

The Hawthorne Effect[7]

Hovering like an invisible cloak over everything that has been said on major accomplishments is the so-called Hawthorne effect. It is there and no one can deny it. It has been a factor in the success of these breakthrough programs which cannot be overlooked. In fact, at most institutions the effect was openly recognized and most of them sought to capitalize on it as a means of enhancing the program's impact. To this extent, the Hawthorne effect contributed significantly to the success of the experimental programs.

MAJOR DEFICIENCIES

Even after the most lavish and successful dinner party, there are leftovers. Perhaps there are leftovers from certain dishes for which more was prepared than could be partaken. Often there are leftovers from dishes which guests did not have the time or take the time to consume. Occasionally, the leftovers are items some did not like or which disagreed with them. So

---

[7] The term used to describe the milieu which somehow pervades an experiment and subtly influences those who conduct it and those who are involved in it. This term is derived from the well-known industrial experiment at Western Electric's Hawthorne plant in Cicero, Illinois.

it is with a successful series of programs of teacher education. Here too, there often are leftovers—things untouched—and for much the same reasons.

While much has been achieved in the forty-two colleges and universities—aided and abetted by venture capital—there is much that remains undone. The major problems largely left unresolved have been grouped into six categories and each will be discussed in the pages which follow.

Reality vs. Dreams

In too many instances, given the "cold, fishy eye" of objectivity, the purposes outlined for a number of the projects were more expressions of hope than of reality. In a word, it would appear that often the institutions' reach exceeded their grasp. In several instances the stated objectives could not possibly have been accomplished within the alloted time with the given resources. In other instances, the objectives simply were unobtainable, even under the most ideal circumstances. The elaborate study on prediction of teaching success at the University of Hawaii is a case in point. More obvious and widespread was the expectation of many programs that the students would be given extensive experiences in team teaching, educational television, programmed learning, and other new techniques of teaching and learning. The hard, cold facts are that this simply did not happen to the hoped-for extent. Notable exceptions are the programs at Harvard, Maine, Pittsburgh, Reed, and Wisconsin, where adjacent school districts either had separate grants for these purposes or already were innovating on their own. On the basis of visits, interviews, data from questionnaires, and institutional reports, it is probably safe to estimate that no more than 10-15 percent of the trainees were involved in working with these innovations in teaching and learning.

Elementary vs. Secondary

As has been indicated already, most of the programs were for the preparation of secondary school teachers. Even in those curricula which included preparation for both elementary and secondary teachers, the major focus usually was secondary and it was here that there were the most candidates. Notable exceptions to this generalization were the projects at George Washington, Michigan State, New York University, and Webster. On the basis of the accumulated evidence on overall impact, the magnitude of the breakthrough must be limited largely to the preparation of secondary school teachers. Hopefully, institutions interested in elementary education will follow the success of Michigan State and George Washington in redesigning the preparation of elementary school teachers. However, interviews with dozens of elementary specialists in the various institutions made it apparent that only the first shots have been fired in the battle to reform the education of elementary school teachers.

The principles of breakthrough programs have been demonstrated. They really could be adopted and adapted by other institutions or by the elementary education faculties of the Ford-grant institutions. But too many of today's Dewey-eyed professors of elementary education—once innovators and pioneers themselves, but now serene and somewhat defensive—can't see the new curricula. "It's fine for secondary," they say, "but it won't work for elementary."

Some new massive drive has to be initiated in the education of elementary school teachers. Where it will come from, and when, is a moot question. In the foreseeable future, it seems apparent that it will not be sparked by venture capital or by a Conant-type investigation. For the time being, perhaps we must be content to conclude that the American people are satisfied with their elementary schools and with the manner in which their teachers are educated.

State vs. Liberal Arts Colleges

Related to the problem of a major reform in the education of elementary school teachers is the fact that the state colleges of America—colleges which only recently were teachers colleges —by and large have not been involved in the Ford-grant breakthrough effort. These are the colleges which have prepared, and will continue to prepare, the great majority of the nation's elementary and secondary school teachers.

The notable exception in the Ford group is Central Michigan. Until the innovating curricula begin to filter down to the state colleges, elementary school teachers likely will be prepared in the Seventies much as they have been since the Thirties, i.e., with two years of general education topped by two years of professionalized subject matter and professional education—the latter dominated by a series of methods courses in every aspect of the elementary school curriculum from arts and crafts and handwriting through reading and rhythms and games. Liberal arts and its proper place in the scheme of the education of elementary teachers have not entered the picture to any great extent. Unfortunately, many liberal arts professors consider the elementary school problem beneath their dignity. The California State Board of Education, in adopting requirements for a liberal arts major for elementary school certification, may have started a trend which could become significant if other state boards were to take similar action.

Liberal Arts Courses

Making more liberal arts courses available to teachers or designing liberal arts courses which are appropriate for them has been an objective of a number of these programs. The Carnegie Institute of Technology is an example of an institution where professors of the liberal arts became interested in teaching courses in their subject areas especially for teachers. Once captured, their interest deepened as they became more involved in pre-collegiate curriculum reform in their respective fields. And, as their contribution to the reorganization of instruction became recognized by the schools, the problem became one of more demand on their time than they reasonably could contribute.

As the director of the UCLA program has pointed out, time is not the only factor:

> As academicians are increasingly involved in pre-collegiate curriculum reform projects, it becomes apparent that universities are not quite sure that this is the right work for academicians. Universities are not at all certain that pre-collegiate curriculum construction fits the concept of university function. . . . Some of the pre-collegiate reform

183

projects which started at the core of the universities have now moved to the periphery or off the campus entirely.[8]

Despite the problems of time and propriety, much more of this needs to be done—by more institutions, by more liberal arts professors, for many more teachers, both pre-service and in-service.

North vs. South, East vs. West

The geographic distribution of the grantee institutions should cause concern among those who live in the West and South. No breakthrough programs have been funded in twenty-four states west of the Mississippi River. The farthest west is Kansas State University until one arrives in Oregon or California. Similarly, with the exception of North and South Carolina, the South and Southwest are "slighted." It is hard to believe that there were neither the personnel nor the climate for mounting projects in all of Texas, Florida, Washington, Minnesota, and Arizona, to single out only a few states which have within them a number of prestigious institutions. The Negro colleges and universities of the South and Southwest also have been excluded at a time when their teacher education curricula largely are still in the teachers college mold.

We can only hope that educators in the neglected states will hear of the results of these forty-two programs, perhaps via such reports as this, and thus be inspired or provoked to initiate experiments of their own.

Theory vs. Practice

Within a number of the forty-two programs there are wide gaps between what ought to be and what is, i.e., *some of the programs or crucial parts of them were not what they seem to be*. Internship has often been grasped as a magic word and used to describe what in reality are student teaching experiences. At the other end of the continuum, in a few instances,

---

[8] John I. Goodlad, "The Academician, Friend or Foe of Teacher Education?" *The Journal of Education*, Vancouver, Canada: University of British Columbia, No. 11, March, 1965, pp. 41-42.

one finds a first year's teaching assignment labeled an internship when in reality it is a good school induction program, nothing more, nothing less. The University of Missouri at Kansas City and Kansas State University are cases in point. The term "seminar" is another example of the use of a magic word, in this case as a cover-up for the usual education courses taught in the usual way. Similarly, numerous instances were encountered in which the integration of theory and clinical experiences was more "talked about" than "done about." As a matter of fact, the really outstanding programs—at Claremont, Cornell, Hawaii, Maine, North Carolina, Northwestern, Michigan State, Reed, Stanford, and Wisconsin, to mention the top ten in this connection—stood out in part because of their notable success in relating theory to practice and practice to theory so that each illuminated the other.

Supervision of interns often was honored more in the breach than in practice. The exact combination of supervisorial resources—institutional and school district—is not easily compounded and much more needs to be done to improve this critical element in these breakthrough programs and others like them.

Many clinical experiences were in traditional school settings, using traditional supervising teachers and principals with their traditional approaches to teaching and learning. To top it off, the kingpin in the supervisorial hierarchy—the college supervisor—too often was likewise rooted in the old way. Hopefully, "gung ho" program directors and innovation-charged interns will change all this in time.

Discipline Center vs. Spiral Center

The organization of professional subject matter (education theory) posed problems in all programs. A few solved the problem by doing business as usual, i.e., using existing courses for interns. In some cases interns and regular students took the same course at the same time. The concept held in such instances was that education content, like the content of any other academic discipline, has an inherent logic and integrity, one which is known only to the expert whose function it is to

185

parcel it out to his students in correct amounts at stated intervals during the semester.

The majority of programs used the discipline-centered approach in teaching social, psychological, historical, and philosophical content in education, but attempted to integrate theory with practice in the teaching of curriculum and methods courses. Usually this integration was accomplished by concurrent enrollment of the student in courses and laboratory experiences, and by having the same person or team of persons teach the "course" (usually called a seminar) and also supervise the laboratory work. In this case, the function of the instructor would be to lead his students into a discussion of their experiences, their questions, and their problems. Thus he utilizes the immediate situation as a springboard into theoretical principles, using the logic of the students to help them gain insights.

A few programs utilized a team teaching approach in which a single group of staff members worked together with a group of students during all (or most) of the twelve- to fifteen-month professional education experience. Such teams usually consisted of a psychologist, a sociologist, and a school curriculum specialist. The team organized and taught the seminars, using the interns' immediate concerns as the point of departure and drawing upon their special fields of knowledge as the situation demanded. Later, when the same or similar problems were of concern, the staff team went deeper into the required theoretical content, building on the interns' previous learning as well as on their additional experience and maturity. Taking a leaf from Bruner, educators have called this type of curricular organization of professional education the spiral curriculum—a curriculum approach particularly suited to the introduction of professional content concurrently with laboratory practice. Its uniqueness meets the criterion that content be of the kind needed, in the right amount, and introduced at the proper time.

What is a spiral curriculum? Imagine a wheel (Figure 1) whose hub is the seminar topic, "planning." This theme was selected because it bears on the problems which interns are immediately facing in the classroom. Broadly interpreted, planning involves all the elements in the teaching-learning situations. The spokes of the wheel are the content areas of

186

teacher education. The curriculum begins near the hub and continues around it in ever-expanding spirals. As each spoke is crossed, information of the kind and in the amount needed is drawn from the content areas and included in the seminar.

How does the spiral curriculum operate? During the interns' first few days of teaching, a 360° swing around the hub, "planning," may be made in a single seminar, with all five of the spokes contributing content to the seminar topic for the day. Other seminar topics follow, such as "implementing instruction" and "evaluating instruction." Complete revolutions daily may soon give way to partial revolutions as the interns are ready for the study of a topic in greater depth. Eventually, the subject content represented by a single spoke ("Learning and the Learner," "Growth and Development," "Curriculum and Instruction," "The School in American Society," or "History and Philosophy") may contribute content for several consecutive seminars. In this way use of the spiral curriculum enabled the staff to guide interns to professional content beyond their immediate concerns but important to their continued growth in professional competence.[9]

Interns taught the usual education courses in the usual way were as critical of them as students often are purported to be of education courses in conventional curricula. But interns taught the spiral way were openly enthusiastic about education courses. However, this enthusiastic response to education courses was limited largely to those few programs where the sequence was a unified "package" program rather than a distinct series of *courses*.

To return to our analogy of the leftovers from the dinner party, the need for reorganization of the theoretical content of education (separate, compartmentalized courses) is one of the biggest leftovers from the lavish and successful party for which the Ford Foundation has picked up the tab.

A Concluding Word

As already indicated, in at least eleven cases the breakthrough curriculum has become the standard curriculum. In a sense, then, it already has become the conventional program that

---

[9] Stone and Robinson, *loc. cit.*

this name implies. In time, it too must be challenged by an as yet unknown innovation or invention. Pending the day when this happens, the approximately 1,000 institutions in America which continue to educate teachers through conventional curricula would do well to consider the curriculum concepts demonstrated by the series of Ford Foundation breakthrough grants in the forty-two institutions. This evidence, added to the earlier success with twenty-eight somewhat comparable programs by the Fund for the Advancement of Education, plus dozens of

Figure 1
The "Spiral Curriculum" Concept

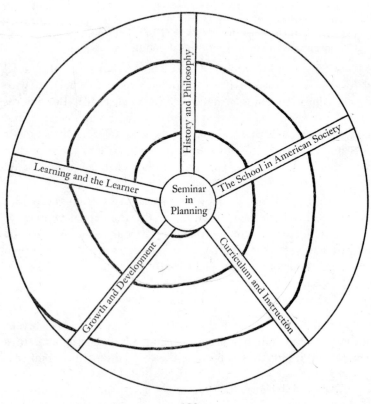

similar ones instituted by colleges themselves, is substantial. In summary, the curriculum concepts demonstrated to be effective and essential include:

1. A four-year liberal arts degree program with professional education usually reserved for the fifth year and culminating in a MAT degree—pre-service for some, in-service for many.

2. Institutional responsibility exercised by supporting faculties in the academic and education disciplines, with subject matter competence emphasized through general and specialized study coupled with or topped by professional preparation.

3. The paid teaching internship, which has been the means of recruiting high caliber liberal arts graduates to teaching, has made clinical practice the heart of the training program, and has made it possible for public school systems to fulfill their indispensable clinical role in teacher education.

4. The continuous integration of theory and practice throughout the professional curriculum, embodying institutional-school district cooperation and utilizing a staff-team which teaches, supervises, evaluates, and guides a particular group of students throughout the professional sequence.

5. A reorganization of the professional content of education courses along some other basis than compartmentalization of separate courses taught by separate instructors, separate from clinical practice.

6. The use, by the prospective teachers, of the newest curricula, the latest materials, the most experimental methods, and the newest techniques and organization for carrying on instruction.

7. High personal, academic, and professional standards for admission to, retention in, and graduation from the program.

8. Multiple pathways to teaching, recognizing the diverse needs of the teaching profession and the varying abilities and backgrounds of those who wish to teach.

Risk capital for experimentation in teacher education began in Arkansas in 1951. Now, fifteen years and 70 million dollars later, what may we conclude? In a word, a breakthrough is under way. Its impact on forty-two institutions and their co-operating schools has been impressive. How long the impact will continue to be felt and where, when, and in what other

189

places, no one can say. How far it will go and how soon it will broadly effect the education of *all* America's teachers depends on the extent to which leaders in other institutions apply the new elements in revising and designing their own programs.

Discussion of the Stone Paper

DAVIES: Ever since I have been in the teacher education field (about twelve years), I have heard much agitated talk about the Ford-sponsored breakthrough programs. When I arrived at Teachers College, one of the first things I was told by a fellow doctoral student was that I would very soon have to choose a side—for or against Ford. He told me that I was going to have to get on the side of those he felt were the "good guys," or I would soon be tagged as a "bad guy." I resisted this advice, because I rather like to consider myself a "middle guy."

Since then I have been unhappy with the amount of time and energy devoted to the politics of choosing up sides. I have been unhappy with a good deal of the behavior of all of the sides. Those promoting the new ideas such as the Ford breakthrough programs have been given too much to the hard-sell approach. Those involved in the conventional programs have spent their time defending what is, rather than looking for useful ideas and new insights in the programs. People have fun seeing themselves as part of the forces of light arrayed against the forces of darkness, but if we want to reform teacher education, more mature and rational thinking is needed.

The "good guys" and "bad guys" syndrome explains in part why the breakthrough programs have not had as substantial an impact on conventional teacher education programs as they should have had.

One of the most exciting points in Mr. Stone's paper is the spiral approach to the curriculum. Mr. Stone's comments take me back to where I started in teacher education—at Adelphi College with Tom Alexander and Agnes Snider, who were leaders at the experimental New College of Teachers College in the early Thirties. At Adelphi we tried to put together a teacher-education program built around the problems of college stu-

191

dents and the problems they would face later as people and teachers. We started with the problem and moved to the theory. Perhaps what we were doing is closely akin to Mr. Stone's spiral curriculum concept.

Some would say that if the professional curriculum is organized in this way professional preparation is reduced to the craft level. Some would say that the spiral curriculum diminishes the intellectual groundings that most of us feel are necessary in teacher education. I don't share these concerns.

A second point worth special attention in Mr. Stone's paper has to do with the close relationship between programs of preparation and the schools. There is some danger in going all the way toward relating preparation and the immediate problems in the schools. If we do go all the way, we may simply be reinforcing the *status quo* in the schools. We may be preparing teachers for the lowest common denominator of school practice rather than for innovation and leadership.

A third item of special interest to me is the question of how to bring about constructive change and reform in teacher education. There are many different theories and many different practices. The effort of the Ford Foundation in the breakthrough program is based on one theory about change. The California legislature apparently had another theory about how to reform teacher education. In the TEPS Commission we have still another: boring from within. We work as an agency of the Establishment with people inside the Establishment to promote the reform of teacher education.

SCHUELER: I'm glad you mentioned the political aspect of this problem. One of the things that bothers me about the political aspect is that there is a tendency in foundation grant-giving to promote what's developed from them as being new, as being breakthroughs, as being experimental, and thereby to cast all else in the shadow as being mere conventional programs that don't do any experimentation, in which there's no development. I think this is most unfortunate because, contrary to what's been said today, often truthfully, there have been many experiments within so-called conventional programs that have followed different patterns. And to consider that there is now a dichotomy in American teacher education, one part being the experimental version (the MAT) and the other being all the rest of us more conventional educators, is just not true to fact. This is preventive, as Mr. Davies has said, of a lot of constructive thought, a lot of getting together of well-meaning professionals. As a matter of fact, I think one of the dangers now is that the so-called new programs have become, in many cases, prematurely cemented with their own conventions, one of them being the concept of team teaching, which is supposed to be so very new and so very experimental. I have heard exponents of team teaching (even from Harvard) present a formula which they indicate should never be deviated from. i.e., in the classroom you have to have a hierarchy in the team. You have the nose-wiper at the bottom and you have the team leader at the top. It's got to be that way or it isn't team teaching. Now, that's why it seems to me that we're getting ourselves into this "either-or" business. Either you do it this way or the rest is out.

There are a lot of things (and here I have to speak in support) that have happened as a result of the stimulation of the Ford MAT programs. They have freed people, and sometimes I worry about how temporarily they have freed them (because, you know, the second generation is coming up)—they have freed people to start afresh and say, "Now give what you've got and let's see whether you can do a better job with it." It's perfectly true, and there's a lot we can learn from it; the next step, however, is not to say that by 1980 we are going to train teachers in this way. I see an entirely different kind of program of training, a bit more of the kind Mr. Bush menioned in his Pattern 1, in which you have a combination of these several worlds. I see nothing wrong with a professional training program that starts before a student finishes his baccalaureate. It seems to me that when a student makes a commitment to teaching is the time when you should start working with him. If he makes his commitment to teaching a little later, you start with him then. You have a program for him then. And at the other end, I would agree completely with Mr. Bush that the process of training should never conclude at the end of whatever formal program you have, whether it's an MAT, an M.S. in Ed., or an M.A. You have to continue your training beyond that with

193

training procedures, concepts, and seminars in the first years of service of the new teacher. And I trust that that's the kind of pattern we're going to use in 1980 to professionalize the training of the teacher.

I've tried to say something that perhaps Harry Broudy would have said (although I'm not in full agreement with him), but I do think one of the problems of the MAT concept is that it has been given a rationale that has two unfortunate aspects to it: 1) that one shouldn't pollute undergraduate liberal arts training with any professional concern (and this was, remember, one of the directives)—you simply don't worry about any of this until the person has gotten his A.B.; and 2) that you are given a very strict time limit and are asked to put the young teacher into a classroom with a minimum of preparation before he gets his feet wet. Now these are concepts which are fine; they are acceptable; but there are alternatives as well. There are many alternatives that one can work on and this is not the only way.

STONE: At the beginning I indicated, you'll recall, that of these forty-three programs six were undergraduate teacher-education programs which I chose not to discuss because we didn't have time. Twelve of them were five- and fifth-year programs with professional studies beginning in the junior year, which I also didn't discuss for lack of time. I concentrated my comments on the twenty-five MAT programs because I think they were most significant. I chose to make my own prediction as a personal one not related to the various alternatives represented in the Foundation's grants, and I would defend this, if we had more time, on the basis that all the developing trends in American education are in this direction. They are going to force more education on all of us.

BELLACK: I think it might be helpful if we relate to what Harry Broudy proposed yesterday and focus attention for a moment on the middle-range theories dealing with problems of practice and the development of theories to guide practice. Now one might reject the importance of the theory-practice relationship and say that teaching is a craft, essentially developed on the spot by rule-of-thumb procedures, etc. Rejecting that posi-

194

tion for the moment and taking the lead from Mr. Broudy's analysis, I suspect that the theory Mr. Stone has been talking about is in large measure developed in the seminars in which the problems of the teacher are related to the various fields of knowledge from which they draw. And the question I would like to raise is the extent to which these programs have attempted to codify this theory, to relate it to research, to get at the questions of how one relates theory to practice. Has any analysis of this nature been made?

STONE: Well, I think there has been some, but I would certainly agree that it hasn't been done long enough and extensively enough and in enough places to have come up with very much. This question is always raised, and it implies a criticism. I think you said, "Do we lose some content here? Do we lose some important piece of knowledge that isn't "covered" because we don't have a systematic outline to go by, etc.?" Maybe this is so. In several of these new programs, all kinds of evidence is collected on what takes place, what kind of content was covered, and from what disciplines the concepts came. The instructors keep tape recordings and they get feedback from the students as to the relevance of the instruction. But your question is always asked, with an implied assumption *that in the old way everything gets covered and everything gets learned*: "When I taught a course in the old way in educational psychology to sophomores about learning, they got it, we covered it, and I know darn well they learned it because I gave them an examination and I graded it and there's the evidence. And then in their junior year I gave them a course in the sociology of education and I know we covered it, too. I am an expert in educational sociology and I gave thirty lectures. They all wrote five papers which were graded and they took a final examination. So they all got it too; they learned it. Three years later when they're in a classroom (or two years later, or the next semester), because they learned it back when, they'll be able to apply it. They knew it at one time and therefore they'll use it now."

I just don't think, from all we know about the forgetting curve, that this has any validity.

195

DAVIES: Mr. Bellack, in order to have a viable professional content, must it be presented sequentially or systematically?

BELLACK: I was not referring to sequence; I was talking about the problem of developing the body of theory every professional group needs to guide practice. And it seems to me that if we had such knowledge we could speak more persuasively, more authoritatively, than if we express merely our own judgments, our own prejudices, and what we like or do not like.

STONE: I agree and I think the next step would be to codify this from all these disciplines in terms of how you grapple with it, whether it's in terms of classroom problems or themes or issues; but how do you grapple with each of these pieces and pull from the various disciplines content which is relevant to the student?

BOYAN: I wonder if anybody has ever made a cost accounting of the resources used to support teacher education at the undergraduate level? What would it reveal to us in terms of unrealized investment? If we do find that a certain proportion of what is invested is unprofitable, we might then think about the possibility of freeing that investment for more powerful use by locating teacher education only at the postbaccalaureate level.

This does not mean that the question Mr. Bellack has raised about the wisdom of codifying our procedures and our theory, etc., is irrelevant. The need is just as powerful if it were located only at one level or the other. My own hunch is that we waste a lot of resources at the undergraduate level. My own hunch is that it permits the continued involvement of many institutions in teacher education that have no business in it and that offer teacher education primarily as a kind of insurance program for large numbers of students who, when undergraduates, are not sure what they are going to do. So I would suggest to you that one of the places we could look to for resources to invest in teacher education (perhaps a way of getting a lot of marginal people out, both students and professors of teacher education) is to consider seriously the location of the professional domain of teacher education at the postbaccalaureate level only.

Now, that's one kind of question the whole Ford-mounted operation helps us to confront, if we want to confront it. It's not a popular thing to confront. Political implications are rampant in it.

The second basic kind of question, an extremely powerful one, is this: Under what rationale and on what basis, related to any kind of responsible training for professional preparation, do we dare place teachers in classrooms with full responsibility on a whole-day basis for a whole year where they have to carry the full load of the teaching and then ask them to apply to this practice what they are learning in the seminars? How can they collect evidence which supports or does not support a particular position or trial? The inundation of the daily job, I suspect, itself interferes with some of the basic notions we want to generate in the related seminars. And, basically, I would then ask this question: To what extent do our existing intern programs serve as substitutes for graduate stipends and to what extent do they really serve as the vehicle for the optimum in teacher education?

MORK: I want to say a couple of things in relation to the discussion here and the function of this symposium. It's excellent that Phi Delta Kappa is providing the forum in which this can be aired, because there have been too many instances where it has not been possible for people to present good sensible papers and others to give good sensible responses. Too often the meetings about some of these programs have been more in the nature of revival meetings, or something of this sort, than anything else. Maybe some of them should have been revivals, that's true. But I'm sure you all understand what I'm getting at, and as Phi Delta Kappans we certainly wish to underline the importance of doing research to test the outcomes of these programs. After all, research is one of the major foundation stones of the fraternity.

We have to be careful at this point that we do not simply ask the Ford Foundation folks to prove the effectiveness of *their* program. Yesterday some of us were responding defensively because we had been asked, in turn, to prove the value of what we are doing, even though no one else has ever been asked to do this. What we want to say is that everybody should

197

remain open-minded, that more data could be gathered or we try to run some experimental programs, not programs that just fit a pattern determined by an armchair decision someplace. We can well get away from terms referring to the usual teacher-education programs as being "dewey-eyed," for instance. This sort of thing is unkind and it's unfair. It's just as unkind and unfair as in the reverse to say that these other programs would sag all over the place if it weren't for their *foundation garments*. We need, as an emerging profession—because this is what we are—to gather data and draw some conclusions that haven't been determined in an *a priori* manner.

STONE: One of the things I didn't get a chance to talk about is the idea of multiple pathways into teaching. I skirted over this, but I tried to indicate that there are all kinds of internship patterns and there are possible patterns not yet invented. The full-time internship is fine for one kind of student, the one-eighth time is fine for another kind, maybe the one-half time for another kind, maybe no internship for still another kind. I think we need all kinds of bright, able people in teacher education. They come to us with individual needs and goals, and we ought to be wise and creative enough to develop programs to fit the needs of these various kinds of people. In other words, at long last I think we ought to do what we've been talking about. In teacher education we've been talking about individual differences among students for 50 years and we've been preparing them as if they were all of one kind. I think it's time we developed training programs that recognize these individual differences through multiple pathways.

DAVIES: Do you include multiple points of entry?

STONE: Yes, multiple points of entry too. You may recall that I said I think *some* students can teach without any so-called professional work. And at the other extreme there are students who may need to be kept two or three years in the teacher-training "hothouse" before our responsibility as an institution may be relaxed.

Now I'd like to say something about Mr. Boyan's idea of resources. Nobody picked me up on this so I'm going to have to say it anyway. I made some reference to the fact that I thought at some point in the future something else other than our present scheme of licensing teachers ought to be adopted, maybe a new kind of device, and maybe an MAT degree might be it. In this state, for example, our teachers spend about a million dollars a year supporting a certification agency which, I would contend, has little or no basis for saying, "These teachers are good and therefore we certify them," or "These teachers aren't and so we don't." It seems to me that we might conceive of the time when California teachers themselves might rise up and say, "This million dollars might better be used as a resource in this and this way for the development of new programs, for experimentation, and whatnot, rather than be used to support a group of people who say, 'This guy had the right courses and this guy didn't have the right courses; therefore, this guy is certified to teach and this one isn't.' "

SCHUELER: May I, just to balance things, say something in support of your spiral curriculum. I'm very much in favor, and always have been, of getting away from the lockstep of the credit system. I'm afraid that in teacher education, in order to seem as respectable as our liberal arts colleges, we have tended to foster it. I've had frustrating experiences going to conventions of the History of Education Society and the Philosophy of Education Society in which the theme seemed to be, How many courses in philosophy of education or history of education, respectively, can we put pressure on institutions to require in teacher education?

I have a letter on my desk from the New York State Reading Association insisting that every prospective teacher, no matter at what level, has to have six credits in reading. The association doesn't say what's supposed to be in it, but it's got to be six credits. We are our own worst enemy in this. Even in adjacent fields I have had great difficulty in getting clinical psychologists and educational psychologists to sit down and talk together, even though they are in adjacent fields. And the real difficulty I see in developing curricula of this type which emerge from the professional need (which I think is where teacher education has to take its cue, from the needs of practice, not from theory) is to get the representatives from the so-called disciplines in teacher education to work together in developing a joint curriculum. The spiral kind is one of them. This, as far as I can see, has been one of the great stimuli of some of these programs, because it has forced people to do this. There is a commitment. You take an appointment in this kind of thing and you are committed to that.

COGAN: I'd just like to propose a hypothesis that this question of the relationship between theory and practice may not be soluble at all if we examine it in the framework of our present training of students. The traditional disciplinary courses in educational psychology, sociology, and anthropology, etc. didn't relate; and Mr. Stone gave us the criticisms of the students; and we all know that your data are reliable here, and we all corroborate it. Furthermore, the students couldn't find a relationship between the systematic courses and the everyday practice. I'm thinking that the same thing will in part be true with the spiral curriculum if we pursue our present course. It would be true, also, if we had a new formulation. The reason is this: The problem of relating theory, speculation, and research to practice is not entirely a problem of bringing the theory, into the practice, in the sense that one teaches theory in the schools. The problem is, in part (that is, in the schools where students are doing student teaching), that we have to get the students to realize their responsibility for moving from theory, which is never practical in the applied sense by definition, to practice, and from practice to theory, *on their own*. If you were to embed a theoretical course in practice, then the students would come up with this perception, "My job is to take the gimmicks that were suggested and find ways of using them in my teaching." Or if you gave them a theoretical course mixed with practice in the sense I'm talking about, they'd come out of the process with a perception that would run something like this: "It is my job to apply the theory, to use the theory and the research, of which I have had several examples, i.e., gimmicks, in the development of my own teaching." So perhaps any of the solutions might work if my students were convinced somehow that it was in large part *their* responsibility to seek these connections rather than waiting for *us* to make the connections, especially in an over-vocationalized form, i.e., forty-eight tricks for motivating fifty-seven varieties of individualized instruction.

That is deadening, too. So maybe we have to use whatever conditions we do have and bend them into new kinds of teaching. We must teach the students to be responsible, in part, for the integration of their own learning.

BELLACK: It seems to me that theory is exactly the opposite of the gimmicks. Theory gives us conceptual frames for analysis and identification of the various factors involved; it never gives one a specific prescription for practice. It is in that sense I was using theory—exactly the opposite of the gimmick.

COGAN: The students who complain about the lack of relationship between theory and practice are in a sense saying, "Please give us a gimmick."

BELLACK: And we have to disabuse them of this.

COGAN: Exactly.

STONE: I think that depends upon the level of student you're talking about.

COGAN: Well, Mr. Stone, we're talking about the very highest level. I just wonder whether if *in actuality* it is ever possible to get enough of the highest level of people each year from our colleges. I mentioned this to Nate Gage while we were listening to you and he said Dael Wolfle's studies of years ago demonstrate that this is probably impossible; I think it would take perhaps the upper half of all our graduates.

STONE: Well, if you think of the present school as thirty little boxes with thirty pupils in each one and the so-called qualified teacher with each of them, we'll never get enough good teachers. But if we're thinking of a whole new conception of the organization of the school and a new conception of the role of the teacher as a coordinator of resources—para-professionals, teacher aides, teacher assistants, readers, and all these things—which is the kind of school I'm talking about—then I think we can get this top priority individual. We *can* get the resource leader with a graduate degree—somebody who has responsibility for the utilization of all these resources for teaching varying groups and sizes.

COGAN: I think the necessity is clearly formulated. You're talking about an élite group; you're not talking about raising the level of a million and a half or two million teachers to this leadership level.

BUSH: It seems to me, Mr. Davies, that we are now about ready to begin our symposium. This suggests that it takes time to put our data on the table, and to see where the important issues lie. I hope that what has been said, and what is published, will open a wider discourse and that there will be some continuity, to enable us to capitalize upon what I think has been a useful focusing of the issue. Mr. Davies in his comments placed his finger on one of the crucial issues: How do you organize the curriculum of teacher education internally? We have had some helpful discussion on it. I think his comment about being careful lest we get too close to the schools and therefore lose perspective is an interesting one coming from him at this point.

DAVIES: I don't think you understood what I said.

BUSH: I think I must have misunderstood! I have not noticed either the colleges or the schools being necessarily on the forefront in this process. It would probably be better not to worry about this at the moment. Where do you mount change? Do you go to the Ford Foundation, or to NCTEPS, or to some other group? We have been working on the theory at Stanford that you go to anyone who will give you some help. We have a little machine that automatically purifies all financial assistance so that it's clean when it comes to us.

There are two problems. One is internal, the curriculum itself. The other is the overall design. Do you have separate courses or an integrated system? We have had both. We had one, then we changed to another, and we have recently changed back. We are not sure yet what is the best way to put things together. We are trying to find some kind of a matrix where the trainee, as he begins his training and as he moves into his first two or three years of teaching, can have his practice critically analyzed by people who are expert in a variety of ways —theoretically and methodologically. Practice does not make perfect. Practice may make a bad teacher. Uncriticized practice may build mediocrity. We are trying to search for a way to obtain constructively criticized practice. We have talked about the foundational people, and we have left out, I'm sorry to say, those who are methodologically and curriculum oriented in each of the subject fields; they are fully as important and as central as the others. We need all together to look at practice. We must be imaginative there and we don't yet have the answer. We are beginning to face the problem. If the "breakthrough" programs have done nothing more than make us willing to face the problem we ought to thank them.

Now, in regard to overall design, I tried to suggest yesterday that we probably needed two or three overall designs. We ought not to have too many. In the past, wherever and whenever a person wanted to enter, we let him. This is what I meant when I spoke of chaos and no internal logic and no internal discipline in the program. I'm perfectly willing to have several programs, but they need to be genuine programs within which we are trying to work. In evaluation, rather than compare one design with another, we need to have programs tightly enough knit, with objectives clearly enough defined, to really conduct research on the elements of the program. I think we are ready to move, but I don't want us to fall back, Mr. Stone, and I know you don't either, into a program where everybody does what he wants to do.

One point we have skirted, and it is unfortunately too late to talk about now. Perhaps, sometime, maybe at the next symposium, we can discuss what to do about those who are half committed to teaching, who wander in and soon wander out. A significant percentage of these are women. This is a touchy subject to discuss, but it needs to be discussed. Shall we develop one program that trains a professional person as well as we know how, and selects for it only those who are genuinely committed and who will stay in the profession? And then have another kind of program for those who think they might want to dabble in teaching, or who want to do something without investing too much in it? This latter alternative would mean different kinds of roles for beginning practitioners. It might be profitable to have a symposium to deal with this tough problem, for as long as we try to put on a half-baked program with people who are half-committed, we are not really going to achieve what we need to.

STONE: We tend to think that having so many women in our programs now is the factor causing all the lack of commitment, the dropping in and dropping out. Well, just one item on these breakthrough programs: Two-thirds of the candidates in these programs which have the holding power I reported to you, this staying power—two-thirds of these people are women. So maybe it isn't just the female problem to the extent we thought it was. There are some other things, and I think they are worth looking into.

MORK: I want to underline something that Mr. Cogan said extremely well on this problem of relating theory to practice. I would like to interject here between theory and practice the concept of the application of *principles*, and I think this is really what we've been struggling with. As an old learning professor, I think it is important for us to recognize that transfer is not automatic. Some people in the craft have a rather low concept of teacher education and have been hoping that people can acquire enough *habits* through practice so they can carry a job. Then there have been too many on the other side who are willing to just teach *abstract theories* and hope that these will be applied. I would like to underline what Mr. Cogan said, that we must get the student to feel responsible for making the applications and, I would add, on the basis of *sound principles*.

* * *

BOYAN: I would personally, and I think for the entire group, like to recognize the special contribution of one young man, namely, Jerry Becker, the president of our local chapter, who organized and administered this whole operation. I think he deserves some very, very fine applause.

DAVIES: On behalf of all of us who are not from this campus, I would like to express our appreciation to the Stanford chapter of Phi Delta Kappa, to Phi Delta Kappa International, to the university, to the School of Education, and to all of you who have extended your hospitality. Professor Richard

Gross, chapter advisor, would like a minute at this point to speak on behalf of Phi Delta Kappa.

GROSS: Mr. Davies and Mr. Boyan have both expressed ideas I wanted to put forth. Certainly on behalf of the international organization as well as Delta Chapter and the School of Education at Stanford, we want to thank all of the discussants and speakers and all of you who attended so regularly and who've all contributed to the spirit of this occasion. I should like to recognize the presence of several members of the Board of Directors and professional staff of Phi Delta Kappa International. I also want to commend local chapter members who helped make this a valuable and worthwhile experience for all of us. People have already been talking about the next symposium, and maybe this is a cue. I doubt if this poor chapter could host an immediate follow-up, but maybe some of you will go back to your chapters with suggestions for a related program and perhaps Phi Delta Kappa would be interested in the continuing opportunity to sponsor such a session. Valuable as these symposia are, however, as Mr. Bush indicated, the real job of thinking our way through some of these key questions in teacher education is going to demand much more than a symposium. If we can only find the time and channels to get groups like this together to spend a good deal of time at these issues, I think we may come up with some of the answers. These answers must be further defined and tested before we come to those ideal days of 1980. But as part of such continuing study and conversation, then, let's hope we can continue with needed symposia such as this.

ADJOURNMENT

Chapter VII

Exciting Prospects:
A Subjective Summary

By DON DAVIES
Executive Secretary
National Commission on Teacher Education
and Professional Standards

Teacher education is not one topic but many topics. Discussions carrying the label "teacher education," such as the symposium reported in this volume, inevitably deal with a remarkable range of subjects. For example, in this book about teacher education the reader finds considerable attention given to such diverse topics as school organization, the nature of teaching and learning, curriculum content and organization in the school and college, the application of technology to educational problems, supervision, career choice and career development, the education of disadvantaged children, and strategies for change in education.

Teacher educators are not one breed but many breeds. The participants in this symposium illustrate this diversity—school teachers and administrators, researchers studying the process of teaching, directors of student teaching, college deans, professors of education, curriculum specialists, professional organization staff members.

Pluralism of content and personnel adds vitality, but it also brings confusion and frustration. Pluralism explains, in part, the lack of fundamental agreement on the problems of teacher education which has been characteristic of the field for a hundred years. People talking together about teacher education are often not talking about the same topics, and they talk with different language, values, and concepts about what schools, education, and teaching are for, what teachers should be like, and what the good life is.

These differences make difficult a coherent and logical discourse and the reaching of closure on problems.

Discussions of teacher education typically open up more questions than they answer. This symposium was no exception. Yet this symposium did contain much more than the usual threadbare arguments about overworked problems.

The participants were able to move beyond some of the stale debates of the past to suggest some exciting prospects. In the pages which follow I shall deal briefly and in a personal and impressionistic way with four of these prospects. I have not attempted to do a comprehensive summary. Some of the ideas are drawn directly from the symposium; some are inferred from the discussions; some are my own.

The four prospects are:

1. More effective relationships between schools and colleges.
2. More relevant preparation.
3. More effective utilization of personnel.
4. More effective strategies for change.

PROSPECT ONE: MORE EFFECTIVE RELATIONSHIPS BETWEEN SCHOOLS AND COLLEGES

Control has always been the issue in teacher education, whether the topic is certification, accreditation, the single-purpose vs. the multipurpose teacher preparation institution, the autonomy and authority of departments and schools of education, student teaching and internships, or the nature of subject-matter majors for teachers.

And control is the central issue in current discussions of school and college relationships. School and college people today will quickly agree with Melvin Barnes that "we have business to do together." As long as the discussion deals with the need for cooperation, communication, and friendly relationships there is little problem. But the control issue emerges as a major block to progress when the discussion departs from the superficialities and niceties and gets to matters of finance, administrative authority, and basic policy making.

Why has genuine collaboration between schools and colleges been so hard to achieve? There are three main obstacles. First, neither side has really wanted genuine collaboration. Second, a conventional and cautious approach to administration has characterized both sides. Third, there have been real or imagined differences in point of view about the nature of teacher preparation, both preservice and in-service.

The prospects are brighter now than they have been before that these obstacles can be removed and that progress toward different and productive relationships between schools and colleges can be made.

Both sides are being encouraged by new federally financed programs to want different relationships. The supplementary centers and the regional educational laboratories provided for in Title III and IV of the Elementary and Secondary Education Act of 1965 provide specific and powerful incentives for school-college collaboration. Appetites for new and genuine relationships are being whetted also by fear on both sides that the other will move unilaterally into new territory, formerly reserved for the other. One example is the fear on the part of some that school systems will bypass the colleges and unilaterally offer preservice teacher training for special programs such as Head Start.

The same forces that are building the desire for collaboration in teacher education on the part of both schools and colleges press toward the development of the kinds of imaginative financial and administrative arrangements needed to make collaboration work in practice. The use of clinical professors jointly hired and paid for by school districts and colleges is one good specific example.

When the first two obstacles have been removed (lack of desire and administrative conservatism), the third (real or imagined difference in point of view about the nature of pre-service and in-service preparation for teaching) will be more easily attacked. The difference in point of view is usually summarized by saying that the colleges favor a sound theoretical preparation and the schools a practical one. Others argue

209

that the difference is between preparation for change (college viewpoint) and preparation for the status quo (school system viewpoint). There is little substance in such arguments. As I suggested earlier, the issue is essentially one of control, not ideology. When schools and colleges agree to new forms of "joint sovereignty" in teacher education as suggested by Morris Cogan, then the ideological problems can be dealt with and solved realistically. The resources of both institutions can be drawn upon appropriately and flexibly. The result can be teacher education programs which are stronger both theoretically and practically and which equip teachers to deal adequately with the here and now at the same time as they function as agents of social and educational change.

Prospect Two: More Relevant Preparation

Does teacher education make a demonstrable difference in how teachers teach? This is the central question in assessing teacher preparation rather than the old either-or arguments about theory vs. practice, pedagogy vs. subject-matter, "foundations" vs. methods.

As he rejects either-or thinking, Harry Broudy offers the reminder that there is no need to choose between high levels of abstraction on the one hand and low-level tricks of the trade on the other. His three-level model (interpretive, interpretive-applicative, and technological) for the professional field of study is a sensible and significant idea for those who are building programs and seeking relevance in training.

One of the primary blocks to providing teacher-training programs which make a difference in how teachers teach has been inadequate understanding of the nature of teaching. The greatly intensified research effort into the nature of teaching in recent years makes it more likely that new theories of teaching will emerge which will serve as the basis for developing more relevant programs of preparation.

The examination of the problems of practice should be the primary source for new understanding of teaching and for more relevant programs of preparation. Indeed, as Robert Bush suggests, the examination of the problems of practice should be-

210

come the central activity for individuals preparing to teach. The primary outcome of such examination for the prospective teacher will be, in Bush's language, "the capacity to be a solver of the problems of teaching."

Brighter prospects for new relevance in training programs lie also in the direction suggested by Herbert Schueler's call for helping teachers to "understand the territory." The events of recent months have uncovered "the other America" and have made a number of educators more aware of the festering problems of the ghetto and the serious inadequacies of much of our typical educational program in meeting individual and community needs in the slums. The need still exists, however, to develop on a widespread basis training programs which will prepare young people for the real world and which will give them the confidence and competence needed to teach in the rural and urban slum schools.

Effective subject-matter preparation is another important side of the training-relevance question. Morris Cogan demonstrates the importance of rejecting the clichés about "good, solid majors" and "excellence" and searching for better questions and better answers to old questions about subject-matter preparation.

The prospects of more genuine cooperation in program planning between educationists and academicians increase somewhat the chances that programs of subject-matter preparation will be relevant and will contribute to the improvement of the educational system.

In many ways the most important breakthrough in making teacher education more relevant will come in widespread reformation in the in-service or continuing education of teachers. When schools and colleges accept the idea that the new college graduate is not a finished product fully equipped to teach, major progress can be made. The great hopes lie in supervised, paid internships for all beginning teachers; planned continuity between preservice and in-service phases; acceptance by school systems of financial responsibility for staff development; new ways to differentiate between career teachers willing to make a full professional commitment and teachers who are transients or who wish to make only a part-time commitment; and provid-

211

ing conditions in the schools which will attract, hold, and encourage talented, effective teachers.

Prospect Three: More Effective Utilization of Personnel

An end to the self-contained teacher in the self-contained classroom is in sight. The prospects are for a widespread revolution in concept and practice of staff utilization. The impact on teacher education and the teaching profession will be profound.

New jobs to be done, persistent shortages of talent, and the special problems in slum schools will lead to the introduction of large numbers of auxiliary personnel in the schools (and eventually also in the colleges). There will be teacher aides, counselor aides, community aides, clerks, playground supervisors, volunteers, student assistants. The proper use of auxiliary personnel has great promise for improving the education of all children and making the job of the teacher more manageable, attractive, and satisfying. On the other hand, if problems of role and training are not solved adequately, the introduction of auxiliaries can be divisive, destructive, and damaging. It is clear that auxiliary personnel should be carefully selected and trained for their work and that experienced teachers and administrators need a substantial amount of orientation and training in ways to work with and utilize auxiliaries properly.

Also of great importance will be the development of new relationships and roles for specialists in the schools—the teacher, the administrator, the social worker, the school nurse, the librarian, the psychiatrist. The former isolation of the teacher will be replaced by a situation in which many specialists work in a variety of ways to do the educational tasks that need doing.

More effective use of personnel will also demand the development of new kinds of roles for people who will provide bridges between theorists and practitioners. There will be a great need, as Harry Broudy suggests, for people who know both the language of theory and the language of practice. Training programs for such people will have to depart radically from present compartmentalized graduate school practice.

212

Educators don't like to admit it, but in the past decade or two stimulation for change has come more from the outside than the inside. Obvious examples of potent sources of outside stimulation are the Ford Foundation and the Carnegie Foundation, Conant's study of teacher education, harsh critics such as Arthur Bestor and James Koerner, new federally financed programs such as Head Start and the Teacher Corps, and the curriculum study projects headed by academicians.

But neither the insiders nor the outsiders have been terribly effective as strategists. We've seen a shotgun blast here, a project there, a thrust and a parry on one front and then on another. There has been very little thoughtfully planned, broad-based, well-understood, and objectively evaluated strategy. This is what is needed; the prospects are brighter that such strategies can now be developed.

For one thing, there is a growing impatience with our old definitions of "insiders" and "outsiders." The fact that ecumenism is "in" these days helps to move us beyond worrying about who has what credentials to speak on which topic. Robert Bush's idea that leadership should come from where "the power and logic of the ideas reside" no longer seems like heresy.

Wider involvement of more kinds of people inside and outside the ranks of the profession will make possible the development of more effective and better understood strategies. There will be less likelihood that plans for change in teacher education will be seen as "plots" rather than "strategies."

The existence of new and larger amounts of money also increases the prospects of more effective strategies for change. Increasing amounts of federal and state money will be available to plan strategies for change and to test alternative strategies. For example, the regional educational laboratories will have millions of dollars for such planning and testing.

* * *

One particularly hopeful note in this symposium was the lack of naive assumptions that there is a single and simple answer to any of the significant questions in teacher education. The simplistic "If we could only . . ." approach was, happily, missing. The participants properly concerned themselves with strategies, with the interrelationships among problems, with ideas needing testing, and with speculation about possibilities, directions, and prospects.

These, then, are a few of the prospects. None will be realized easily or completely. Many of the old debates and hostilities and clichés will remain, but alongside the complexities and frustrations and difficulties there are new hopes.

The participants in this symposium recognized the new hopes and the new prospects by looking ahead rather than backward and by moving beyond some of the most familiar arguments of the past.